ENTREPRENEURSHIP EPIDEMIC

The Fever and Its Cure

BHAVESH BUDDHDEV

STARDOM BOOKS

www.StardomBooks.com

STARDOM BOOKS
A Division of Stardom Publishing
and infoYOGIS Technologies.
105-501 Silverside Road
Wilmington, DE 19809

Copyright © 2022 by Bhavesh Buddhdev

This book is copyright under the Berne Convention.
No reproduction without permission.
All rights reserved.

The right of Bhavesh Buddhdev to be identified as the author of this work has been asserted by him in accordance with sections 77 and 78 of the Copyright, Designs and Patents Act, 1988.

FIRST EDITION JUNE 2022

STARDOM BOOKS

A Division of Stardom Alliance
105-501 Silverside Road Wilmington, DE 19809, USA

www.stardombooks.com

Stardom Books, United States
Stardom Books, India

The author and publishers have made all reasonable efforts to contact copyright-holders for permission, and apologize for any omissions or errors in the form of credits given. Corrections may be made to future editions.

ENTREPRENEURSHIP EPIDEMIC

Bhavesh Buddhdev

p. 264
cm. 13.5 X 21.5

Category:
BUS025000 - Business & Economics : Entrepreneurship
BUS060000   Business & Economics : Small Business - General

ISBN: 978-1-957456-06-5

DEDICATION

This book is dedicated to my parents who have always been supportive of all my endeavors. My father, Dhanvantrai Buddhdev has been a guiding light in my life and taught me the essence of hard work, perseverance and business ethics. I dedicate this work to my mother Rasila Buddhdev who inculcated the pill of punctuality into me and to my wife Sangita Buddhdev who has provided unconditional support throughout my entrepreneurial journey. And lastly, this book is dedicated to all the wantrepreneurs who wish to be the harbinger of change.

CONTENTS

ACKNOWLEDGMENTS		i
FOREWORD		iii
INTRODUCTION		1
PART 1: THE ART OF DOING BUSINESS		5
1	CROSSING THE CAREER CHASM	7
2	WHO DARES, WINS!	31
3	PARTNERING THE RIGHT WAY	65
PART 2: STARTUP ESSENTIALS		89
4	STARTUP: WHO? WHAT? WHERE? HOW?	91
5	THE COFOUNDER CONUNDRUM	119
6	THE FUNDING OF STARTUPS	135
7	STARTUP: BEING THE BOSS IS NOT EASY	171
PART 3: THE KEY TO EFFECTIVE PLANNING		191
8	SUCCESSION PLANNING: PREPARING BUSINESS FOR FUTURE	193
9	THE BUSINESS OF GENERATING EMPLOYMENT	215
10	FIND A GENUINE INVESTOR	233
	CONCLUSION	245
	REFERENCES	247

ACKNOWLEDGMENTS

I am indebted to Vaishnavacharya Shri Dwarkeshlalji Maharaj from Vadodara and Late Shri Haricharandasji Maharaj from Gondal for helping me find myself. I show my gratitude to Sadhguru for honing my spiritual instincts.

As I commence on my writing journey with this book on entrepreneurship, I would like to thank my first ever Angel Investor, my uncle, CA Jayesh Buddhdev, Chairman, Meridian Infotech Ltd. My entrepreneurial journey would not have been possible without his initial support. I extend my gratitude to my friend and my first formal partner, Mr. Devang Jasani, without whom my dream company, Meridian Infotech Ltd. would not have reached where it is right now. Mr. Chetan Chug, Founder of Somika Group and my brother-in-law have been a huge support system in my personal and professional growth.

I am grateful to Siddhant and Chintan, my sons for their insights and inputs in every segment of this manuscript. Our joint sessions of watching Shark Tank episodes always encouraged me to invest in startups. I thank my brother Mehul Buddhdev and my first cousins for their support. A special mention to my friend, Bharat Kodinaria, Director, Excelsource International Pvt. Ltd., and to my cousin, Hiren Khakhkhar, Co-Founder, 5Point Solutions Pvt. Ltd. and Mr. Kartikey Hariyani, Founder, TecSo Charge Zone Limited. I also extend my gratitude to my partners, Bharat Bhimjiyani and Nirav Desai for their unconditional support. My transformation from an entrepreneur to an Angel Investor and Mentor would not have been possible without the esteemed guidance of Dr. Apoorva Ranjan Sharma. I am thoroughly indebted to him for introducing me to the world of Venture Capital Eco System.

Last but not the least, every endeavor of mine has seen the light of the day because of the unconditional love and support of my childhood friends, Samir Desai, Utpal Bosmia, Atul Charadva and Dr.Jitesh Parekh. I thank everyone; my friends, my coworkers and staff for their continued love and support. I would like to extend my gratitude to Mr. Raam Anand, Ms. Atrayee and the whole team of Stardom Alliance for their efforts.

FOREWORD

It is indeed a great pleasure, privilege, and honor to write a foreword for a book like Entrepreneurship Epidemic, which is no less than a complete and comprehensive guide for anyone who wishes to step into the world of doing business.

A first-generation entrepreneur, Bhavesh Buddhdev has been a great friend for more than 18 years. Honestly, it was a pleasant surprise when I learned about him writing a book on entrepreneurship. A man who has been excellent with investments in future technologies and progressive ideas is certainly the most appropriate person to guide the younger generation. In my academic capacity, I have always found the younger breeds to be hungry for doing something of their own. Building a startup and choosing to be an entrepreneur has become more like an epidemic where every second person wants to take the plunge. But then, I see very few succeeding because of the absence of proper handholding and guidance.

As I received the draft and turned the pages, I could relate it to every step of my entrepreneurial journey, and so you will. I wish I had this book during my initial days of entrepreneurship. Every page unfolds excellent suggestions and strategies to build a startup successfully. In present times, you can find many books on the topic; however, not many cover the different aspects of building a startup. This book not only helps in building the business but in executing a succession plan.

The book takes you on a roller coaster ride of handling success and failures while playing the role of friend and philosopher in many instances. I have rarely come across a book that deals with the entire life cycle, which informs about the current ecosystem and funding sources. A wonderful compilation of case studies and relevant quotes allows the readers to introspect on every minute of doing business and keep them motivated during difficult times.

Lastly, I can confidently vouch for this book as it encompasses the wisdom of an ethical businessman, a wonderful human, and a passionate entrepreneur. Entrepreneurship Epidemic will be considered Geeta for everyone.

Anyone who wishes to dive into the unchartered waters of entrepreneurship; anyone who has been infected with entrepreneurship fever, this book is your perfect cure.

Best Wishes,

Daulat Singh Chauhan
Pro Chancellor, ITM University.
Gwalior, India

Bhavesh Buddhdev is always full of energy. More often known as BDB amongst his friends, I have always found him ready for the next big thing. BDB is an entrepreneur who has never been worried or scared of risks and challenges. In a proverbial way, he proves that where there is a will, there is a way. In this book, he sounds bold and blunt while teaching the budding entrepreneurs about the challenges of entrepreneurial life. Bhavesh Buddhdev is a true follower of working 24/7 and is always on the run to find the next best business. Entrepreneurship Epidemic reflects that there is no right age or time to start your own business. If you are not happy with your present work and wish to take a plunge into the world of business, this book is your best guide to get in touch with the right amount of knowledge and funding sources. BDB is great at networking and building relationships. May this book Entrepreneurship Epidemic be the start of his writing journey, and I wish the best for his readers.

Best Wishes,

Chetan Chug
Chairman, Somika Group
Democratic Republic of Congo

INTRODUCTION

Once a student asked Elon Musk about the most significant tip for a budding entrepreneur. The founder of Tesla and SpaceX who had been bestowed with a fair share of criticism gave a wonderful response. Musk said, "It is indeed difficult to start a company. It is painful; much more than eating glass and staring into the abyss. If you are wired to do it, then only do it, not otherwise. If you need inspiring words from others, then Don't Do It!"

In a thriving economy like India, opportunities gush out from every nook and corner; one just needs to have the right lens to analyze and grab the situation by its collar and make a profit out of it. Being a part of the largest democracy in the world, we harbor a queer blend of pride, prejudices, and pitfalls. More than 50 percent of India's population are below the age of 25 and more than 65 percent are below the age of 35. Compared to Japan and many other European countries, India's workforce gets a competitive edge due to the age factor. However, with the growing percentage of highly qualified and skilled people, it becomes difficult for a handful of authorities to remain the only job providers. As per the global statistics, India has become one of the fastest-growing startup ecosystems. Moreover, as I pen down this book, more than 89 entrepreneurs have paved their path to becoming Unicorns. The numbers are rising at a faster pace than ever anticipated. On one side of the coin, owning a business and leading a life of an entrepreneur gives one immense power to script one's own destiny.

While on the darker side, every business owner rides on an inescapable cycle of highs and lows. India is rich within its cultural realms and no one can deny that there is a social influence on every young mind while choosing a career. A stable government job provides the best guise in the job market, while a nine-to-five corporate job, too, is bound to occupy your thoughts.

But all said and done, there is no better feeling than becoming your own boss. Conceiving an idea and then trying it out a hundred times without any fruitful result can sound terribly discouraging to some people. But believe me, there is a whole gang of enthusiastic innovators who are running through this daily grind only to eventually bring in a valuable disruption in the system. Even at this very moment, as you turn this page, there is someone, somewhere, pondering upon an existing problem only to find out a solution. And that is called the entrepreneurial spirit. Presently, we Indians are at a point where JF Kennedy's quote makes absolute sense to us. *Ask not what your country can do for you. Ask what you can do for your country.*

It indeed feels safe to be cocooned in a comfortable job while reporting your daily outcome to a mentor. It indeed feels good to have an appreciation in the boardroom and become the employer of the year. However, there is no greater joy than wearing the garb of a job-giver. There is no pride stronger than the pride of contributing to your country's economy.

An entrepreneur's life is always on a roller coaster. At one moment, you will be riding the high of a newly launched product while in the very next moment, you will end up losing a few of the best talents in the team. It is a 24/7 job to find the right balance between business and life as you juggle to prevent your business from sinking.

Erecting a startup and making it grow in the market is going to bring you a blend of inspiring and challenging days. But believe me when I say this—even though a business owner is riddled with hurdles and challenges, the joy of overcoming those is boundless. Choosing business as a career needs strong shoulders as running a business comes with enormous responsibility.

ENTREPRENEURSHIP EPIDEMIC

And as one chalks out an effective business strategy in this flourishing market of entrepreneurship, one is halfway closer to tasting the sweet fruit of success. A good salesman spirit is of the essence for a successful business. If one is determined to turn one's passion into a profession and learn the brass tacks of pursuing business, there is no better career choice than starting your own business. As India celebrates January 16 as National Startup Day, it is a wake-up call for every fence-sitter to cross the chasm of hesitancy and see business as a lucrative career option.

Are you still fearing to take the plunge? Fear Not! Let us dissect every element of running a business and very soon, you are sure to be bitten by the emerging entrepreneurship bug.

PART I

THE ART OF DOING BUSINESS

1

CROSSING THE CAREER CHASM

"The ladder of success is best climbed by stepping on the rungs of opportunity."
— Ayn Rand

Are you a fresh graduate wandering confused about your career path? Have you ever given a thought to starting a business? In the 21st century, the only thing that remains constant is change. It may be a perfect example of an oxymoron, but it is a fact.

Every day, humankind is thrown new challenges, and a new bunch of fresh young graduates comes up with a unique breed of solutions. We are thriving in a time when there is a constant urge to better our livelihoods in every possible way. When you hear the term *livelihood*, the first thought that captures your mind will be your career graph. India has the second-largest population in the world and has a higher proportion of the younger generation. While having a secured job in a renowned company is certainly a pliable desire for every fresh graduate, the world of entrepreneurship can promise a lucrative career as well. I am sure that most would agree that education forms the premise of our knowledge. Then our career path is about applying the gathered knowledge.

But what if a freshly graduated software engineer finds it a little offbeat to design new software codes for someone else? It is not like he is against having a supervisor; he, however, wishes to take the leap and start his own company and design something unique toward solving an existing problem in the current scenario.

Well! Is that acceptable or even conceivable by the world around? Is it acceptable for anyone in the riffraff to take a plunge into this ever-growing ocean of doing business? My answer would be loud and clear. YES. ANYONE CAN DO BUSINESS. Let me enlighten you with the benefits of starting a business. I call it the **7 Wonders of Doing Business.**

- You own your time and remain the decision-maker.
- Unlimited opportunities for income as you unbind your creative hooks.
- Did you know that entrepreneurs are happier and healthier than salaried people?
- Generally, entrepreneurs' lives are satisfying as they enjoy their work.
- You feel more motivated to do what you like in life.
- You choose your lifestyle.
- You become a JOB-GIVER.

Then what is stopping you from taking the plunge? While a young mind can be willing to encash on his entrepreneurial itch, the prying eyes of society always have a say on his career choice. We do grow up in a cocoon of preconceived notions.

A doctor's child is expected to become a better doctor than his parents. It is almost a shame if an engineer's son does not venture into the same career chasm. A similar tone is also applied to a business family; the next generation must keep the legacy going. That is how our human society has grown to date—by continuing the legacy. One's background greatly influences one's education and career selection. Humans are inherently biased and often universalize things. Parents' failure frequently instills fear amongst the next generation.

ENTREPRENEURSHIP EPIDEMIC

If a father has failed in his pursuit of business, he often encourages his children to secure a government job that will never hinder the cash inflow. We hardly generalize success but often waste our precious time pondering upon chances of failure. We all harbor a tremendous ability to get what we must have; nevertheless, we often get lost between 'must' and 'want'.

"A single conversation across the table with a wise man is better than ten years of mere study of books."
- Henry Wadsworth Longfellow

Before I take you all on the roller-coaster journey of pursuing business as a career, let me brief you all on the crux of doing business.

What Is A Business?

The term business refers to an organization or an enterprise engaged in commercial, industrial, or professional activities. So, if you are sitting on the fence about your career, you can imagine the plethora of opportunities you will get. Businesses range in scale from sole proprietorships to international corporations and can range in size from small to large. However, I shall let you all know that even a business giant like Amazon started with a one-room cubicle.

Business is about turning your passion into profit, which in turn can solve some of the prevailing economic and social issues. As a serial entrepreneur myself, I have never encountered anything called the right or wrong motivation for wanting to start your own business. Whether one is trying to escape the nine-to-five work shifts or just wanting to make more money, every reason seemed valid for me. However, there prevails some particular elements which help in shaping a business career.

"Life is a matter of choices, and every choice you make makes you."
- John C. Maxwell

Are You Fit For Business?

Today, India is shining bright as the new ground of innovative ideas. With a growing population and increasing number of highly qualified individuals, governing bodies are falling short in allotting jobs for everyone. We are not struggling with an economic crisis; however, the crisis in the job market is quite daunting, to say the least. As for whether you are fit for doing business or not, it highly depends on your upbringing, social and economic ambiance in the house and family, social circle, etc. On the same note, one's behavioral characteristics, inherent nature of risk-taking or risk-aversion, communication skills, introversion or extroversion, degree of enthusiasm, and ingrained passion toward achieving the goals contribute more to shaping one's business skills.

In my decades of experience, I have often seen youngsters harboring the doubt of plunging into business. Why? Because they do not carry a legacy. Moreover, they not only lack guidance but also proper motivation. There is always a beginning for everything. Change does not happen on its own. Someone has to be the instigator to bring about the new dawn, do something different, and pursue a path never followed before. So, if we return to the basic question, you are fit for business if you are passionate about your business goals. You are fit for business if you can sell anything from a pen to an airplane and if you are ready to learn the nitty-gritty of business right from the crux of it. But, once you decide to escape the rigmarole of the nine-to-five secured job structure, you must be prepared to give your 24 hours toward pursuing business.

Pursuing business as a career indeed makes you your own boss. At the same time, if you wish to see your business progress every day, you must work harder and smarter with each passing day. The influence of parents in the career guidance process is quite elaborate. Parents serve as a major influence in their children's education and in deciding on a specific career. Honestly, parents want their children to find happiness and success in life and be safe in whatever career they choose. The ambiance in a house plays a crucial role.

Let me give an example about Indian upbringing. Gujaratis and Rajasthanis are two groups found to be implicitly indulged in business. Most parents in these states are self-employed, thus inculcating the same habit of starting or continuing a business. One may point out the sound financial background as the main reason; however, that financial stability was not gained overnight. Generations after generations have slogged to build a business empire. Look around; whether it is Ambani or Birla, a generation struggled to build the premise, and the next generations carried the legacy forward. That is how a business thrives.

Similarly, the family ambiance in Bihar or Bengal or Odisha coaxes younger minds to join civil services. The younger generation is taught about the prestige of traveling in an official cavalcade of SUVs with the flashy red light on the roof. In contrast, the southern part of India sees an undying urge to join an MNC and get a green card from the USA. I am not proclaiming any of these ideologies as wrong. However, what if your predecessors' career choices do not influence you? What if you fail to succeed in those competitive examinations or do not get placed in an MNC after graduation? Is there no other door open for your career?

You do have an option! You can hop on to a traditional business or become an entrepreneur; the present demands employment creation. The main aim of this book is to implant the idea of generating employment by choosing business as a career. A business comes with the power of generating revenue and wealth not only for the owner and his family but also for every person associated with the business. Switching to business indeed comes with its own perks and perils. Still, I would say the satisfaction of owning a business overweighs the challenges. *High risks often result in high rewards.*

Considering the present framework of the job market, you can analyze your abilities by asking the following questions:
- ➢ Do you have Sales Skills? Are you an Introvert or Extrovert? Can you convince the world of your thought?
- ➢ Do you have a flair for solving a burning problem of society? Do you possess a problem-solving attitude?

> Do you have any financial backing? Have you lined up any family members or angel investors to initiate the proposed business plan?
> If not anything, are you willing to become an Intrapreneur in any fledgling ongoing business?

Let me tell you, even if you do not possess all the four points currently but have the quality of a skilled salesman, you are a PERFECT FIT for doing or starting a business.

Business Is An Art; Are You In For It?

No success is final, and no failure is utterly fatal. The secret of doing business lies in your passion for bringing about change. Not everyone has to wake up and jump into the trend of startup or entrepreneurship. Widening the scope of your family business, adding new features, and crossing the barriers to go online are also a part of doing business. As social media and the concept of online retail stores have emerged, doing business online has become the new trend for every business, whether startups or traditional companies.

However, the growth of entrepreneurs is not limited to online business. And this condition is universal. Deciding to go into business is a leap of faith. It requires you to push yourself out of your comfort zone and try something new. Business is ever-evolving, and you must constantly churn your creative instincts. That is why Business is an art worth pursuing. Before we delve into the pursuit of startups, let me detail the benefits again.

> **It is motivating.**
> Working for someone else may fetch you a lumpsum salary, but your best potential comes out while working for your own self.
> **You are your own boss.**
> Owning a business is about becoming your own boss.

It imparts the ability to direct the culture of your company. It is like sitting in the driver's seat where you are deciding how best to steer your company into the future. I will not lie; sometimes it is overwhelming, and one must know when and how best to delegate tasks. However, when you can make your own decisions about how best to operate on a day-to-day basis, this leads to creating a culture, a brand, and an organization.

- **Financial independence.**
  Running your own business has several financial benefits over working for a salary. Firstly, you own a company that has the potential for growth. It adds to your wallet as your company grows. Secondly, your business itself is a valuable asset. As your business grows, its worth in the market increases too. You may decide to sell it or hold on to it and pass it down to your heirs. Either way, it is valuable.

- **You can enjoy a flexible time schedule.**
  You can build your own work-life balance. One of the most prominent benefits of owning your own business is the flexibility that comes with it, whether that be working from wherever you want, setting your own hours, wearing a nightgown, or even sitting next to your pet while you work.

- **Your job and income are secured in your own hands.**
  You shape your bank balance once you own your own company. The secret mantra is effective management of funds to make a profit while widening your business domain.

- **You become multitalented.**
  You might have started a business with just a skill in sales. But as your business grows, you come across people from different backgrounds with their unique skills. Over time, you get a good grip over manpower management, efficient financial distribution, organizational skills, technological skills, etc.

- **Scope for unlimited creativity.**
  Whether you start your own business with a unique idea or continue to be a part of your family business, you are on the path of creating something new and something better.
- **You become an employer and serve society.**
  You no longer remain a mere taker in society: you contribute by shaping the job market.
- **You choose the people you want to work with.**
  When you work for someone else, you rarely get to choose with whom you work. If you do not like your colleague or the prevailing work culture in the company, you start looking for a new job. However, the scenario is different when you own your business, since you remain the decision-maker. As you know your business requirements better than anyone else and you possess the authority, you can decide on what kind of talent you need to hire for your company.
- **You take the risk and you reap the rewards.**
  Owning a business is like a game of cricket. To hit a six, you must be prepared for a bouncer. And the more boundaries you hit, the closer you are to victory. No business can be immune to risks. Even if you run a grocery shop, you must brace yourself for the changing demands in the market.
- **No red-tape culture.**
  Business is often unchained from red-tape culture. Of course, an organizational hierarchy is needed to run any business smoothly. Still, while you own the business, you can get things done faster as you need not wait for files to get signed and approved in a bureaucratic way.
- **The pride of ownership.**
  One of the biggest differences in owning your own company instead of working for someone else is the sense of pride you establish in building something of your own. I can borrow the term self-actualization from Abraham Maslow while highlighting this point. And another added feather is that people will be interested in your story.

We live in an era where every day knits a new kind of problem: social, technical, or a pandemic like Covid-19. We must stand up to be productive rather than just being busy. As H. Jackson Brown Jr. quoted, *"Nothing is more expensive than a missed opportunity."*

Is Entrepreneurship The New Normal?

Your parents do not own a business, yet you want to start a business independently? Why? Because you can see a problem that the others have invariably overlooked. The best way to explain this statement is to talk about the businesses that prospered during the Covid pandemic. India went into complete lockdown in April 2020. Shops were closed, restaurants were shut, and people were restrained from going out. Companies like Zomato, 1mg, and BigBasket were not born during the pandemic; however, the idea of delivering the essentials to your doorstep worked wonders for the common citizen as well as the companies.

Let me assure you here, a business is first conceived inside your mind and then comes to the market. To begin, one must prepare oneself financially and emotionally. The idea of doing business is more crucial than having a brimful of money to invest. The product or service you wish to propagate must have a unique quality to make it stand out in the market. Your passion to innovate and tolerance for risk are the major points that help you run a successful business. **Entrepreneurship** is a process of designing, beginning, and running a new business, and the company that offers new products or services is called a **Startup Company**. One must understand that entrepreneurship is not about just coming up with a new idea for a business. A startup needs **24/7 involvement** to widen the scope of doing business and reach clients and customers in an affordable and effective way. Simply put, we can say that **Entrepreneurship is about creating new things rather than sticking to conventional jobs and the traditional mode of doing business.** Thus, a person who sets up a business by taking financial risks in the hope of profit is an **entrepreneur**.

Innovation is the key credential of an entrepreneur who is more of a job creator than a job seeker. Today the biggest challenge before Indian youth is to build the country as a global economic giant. And in this pursuit, the most obvious questions hover around—Why should we become an entrepreneur in India? Why should we not work as part of a larger organization where the opportunities and resources to scale ideas are probably far greater?

Before I answer the first question, let me enlighten the readers with the answer for the latter. The doubt is valid and also possible to attain. There is a famous saying that business or management is difficult to be taught or spoon-fed. One must learn by keen observation and develop the faculties of different aspects of doing business. One needs more than hefty educational degree certificates. Field experience gives a better understanding and illumines an aspirant to the marrows of business. Have you thought of becoming an **Intrapreneur**? It is a specialized job profile where one acts as a manager in an existing business and supervises and nurtures innovative ideas. As I said earlier, a salesman's skill is necessary to dream about starting a business.

A business aspirant can always join the sales team of an existing business to get a good grasp of the market. Understanding the clients and customers, realizing the budding demands in the market, and noticing the competitive grounds and the escape routes are some of the added benefits to be garnered if you join a company before planting your own business ideas in the market. You are free to choose your field.

However, from my experience, I would suggest looking into the market for consumer goods and consumer durables. Once you understand the different variables associated with your chosen field/brand, you can begin your business career by taking a dealership of the product/service you have been marketing successfully. Investing a couple of years in the sales and marketing department will hone your business skills to an appropriate level to start your own journey as an entrepreneur.

ENTREPRENEURSHIP EPIDEMIC

The famed American psychologist Abraham Maslow had a famous quote for the human mindset, "*You will either step forward into growth or you will step back into safety.*" Thus, the decision is always yours: take the risk and explore a path never traveled before or remain protected inside your comfort zone.

> *My beginning too was quite humble. I was from a family with a business background where my father had a textile factory in Saurashtra—Jetpur. I was brought up in a joint family where every other person was into business, but I was not sure of my career choice. In fact, I was the first person to join the Science stream and pursue a degree in Electronics Engineering at MS University of Vadodara. At that point, I could not fit myself into any specific career. And I am sure that even today, every young graduate wander for a while to discover what suits them the best. There was a hue and cry over going to the US for a Master's degree during my college days. Like every other final year student, I too joined the bandwagon and cleared GRE and TOEFL and got admission to one of the universities. However, my mother and grandmother did not allow me to go, and I dropped the plan. Once the glorious USA plan was canceled, I thought of venturing into business. Though I had grown up amid a complete business ambiance, I failed to start anything concrete even after four to five months of effort. Every other member in my family had carved their own line of business, and soon I realized that I too had to make a niche of my own based on my own abilities. Instead of wasting more time, I sat for my campus placement and joined a TV manufacturing company in Maharashtra as a QC Engineer. But within seven months, I realized that it was not my cup of tea and came back to Vadodara.*
>
> #

My professional bent too was highly influenced by the ambiance in which I was brought up. While working in that TV manufacturing company, I read through several business magazines and articles and found one common point in every successful business. SALES. Success in business lay in sales. One can manufacture the best quality of preserved food or develop the most efficient paying app; however, the product or service's success lies in one's skill in sales. Introverts can be good copywriters for your marketing strategy; still, you need an extrovert to make the sales in the field.

Anyway, I took my baby steps in the world of business with a sales job in a Wipro PC dealership. This experience provided me with the much-needed impetus to develop my business skills. Within 10 months, I resigned and took up a Wipro Dealership instead. One of the service partners of Wipro came with me as a business partner. I chose the responsibility of generating sales while my partner was more inclined toward funding and execution. That was my first positive encounter with business, and it gave me the right pedal to move ahead and choose business as a professional career. Within two years of hard work, I could see my profit-making abilities and was thus assured of my career path. Running a business was my deal, and I was on the right path. However, with my present business, my area of operation was limited. I wished to widen my scope, so I started a new company with a partnership with IBM. And there, my own company took birth: **Meridian Infotech Private Limited.** It took me a couple of months to realize where my passion lay. And then again, for a couple of years, I worked hard to understand the brass tacks of doing business. Time, devotion toward your desired goal, and thorough business planning and strategy and its execution are the essential ingredients to make any business successful. After having spent so many years in the business world, I have a single piece of advice for the younger generation. Never fear to take the initial plunge into business, whether traditional or a startup.

ENTREPRENEURSHIP EPIDEMIC

Why So Much Noise About Startups?

You might be reading my book on your Kindle device. Let me ask you—did you ever think of something like a Kindle device or Audible to read a book? Could you think of Google Pay a decade ago? As a child, could you ever think of having delicious food from a well-known restaurant delivered to your own house? No. You would not have thought it possible, but someone did. Even now, at this very moment, when you are reading through my book, I can assure you that more than a thousand minds are busy chalking out their idea of solving a problem that you are unable to see. And that is how the concept of **STARTUP** takes birth. Every development starts with a problem. Every business starts small. As Steve Jobs said, *"It is not the customer's job to know what they want."* Any common individual can become an entrepreneur once they carry a unique lens to examine an existing problem.

The entire world remembers the iPhone's unveiling on January 9, 2007, as the game-changing moment in the world of technology. But during that same year, Amazon announced the Kindle, the first generation of a device that would change the way we read and publish eBooks. In 2004, Bezos thought of a new digital strategy to compete with Apple, which was on the top of the game, thanks to the massive success of the iPod. At that time, Apple also had a huge impact on music, something Bezos wanted to replicate in books. He wanted to control the end-to-end customer experience like Apple did. After many discussions, Bezos decided to focus on being a bookseller in the digital world. Bezos saw an opportunity in eBooks as the future of bookselling.

On the same note, let me remind you India has become one of the fertile grounds for prospering minds in the pursuit of opening startups. The founder of OYO Hotels and Homes, Ritesh Agarwal, became the world's youngest self-made billionaire after Kylie Jenner in February 2020. Ritesh Agarwal realized the poor accommodation system at a given budget in India and conceived OYO Rooms to provide people with an aggregator of bed stays with breakfast.

Similarly, Zomato started with the name of Foodiebay, which was an online restaurant directory. There were days when we used to call different restaurants to place orders and again call up for corrections and directions and reservations. Then came applications like Zomato, which reversed the whole scenario and made it extremely simple for the consumers. Deepinder Goyal and Pankaj Chaddah founded Zomato in 2008, further aiding this process of eating out and food delivery. *Whether they want to change the world or simply make their business vision a reality, the startups are designed to give society something it needs but does not know it yet.*

Startups are conceived with a problem-solving attitude. Startups are young companies founded to develop a unique product or service, bring it to the market, and make it irresistible and irreplaceable for customers. Startups are grounded for innovation and address the deficiencies of the existing products or create an entirely new category of goods and services. Startups often disrupt the deep-seated ways of thinking and doing business for entire industries. Do you remember how the declaration of demonetization changed the whole scenario of financial transactions? Problems come to our life to open new doors of opportunities. It depends on how we perceive the problem and take action against it.

Is There A Right Age For Business?

Never live a life regretting the chances you did not take. It is never worth it. Believe me, we are all given a jigsaw puzzle of our strengths, weaknesses, opportunities, and risks. It is we who have to arrange the puzzle productively. Although there are no set age criteria to begin a business, the age bracket for starting a business has been divided into three categories.

The Early Birds: An indisputable factor distinguishes the younger generation in their early 20s. They are fresh graduates, full of enthusiasm, and carry undying energy to bring about a change. They hold a different lens to see the world and its problems.

Plunging early into business is just a matter of having the spirit of curiosity to try something extraordinary to make a difference. Have we not heard about Tilak Mehta? He is just 16 and is the founder of an app-based courier service in Mumbai known as *Papers n Parcels*. It is a digital courier company that provides one-day parcel services in collaboration with the Mumbai Dabbawalas.

Good sales skills and financial backing are needed to start a business early in your career. It becomes an added advantage if you have enough financial backing from your family or if your family is into business. The process begins with learning basic business skills. Even if you fail to develop a unique idea to start your own business, you can always join your family business to understand the tactics. You can always enter the family business and improve on the topline and the bottom line with fresh thinking.

However, if you find the family business too organized to bring anything new, you can look into a different line of business. I, for example, did not start my business career with my father's textile company. The trick here is to get an experience of four to five years in a new line of business by working with/under someone and then switch to your new venture. And if you have a great idea to contribute to the general public and are well-skilled in sales, there are several modes of securing funds like Angel Investors, Venture Funds, etc. The younger age group is more into developing technology and internet-based startups. However, innovation is never restricted under an age bracket. You are allowed to wait to gain experience and financial stability before deciding to take the plunge.

Pros: Enthusiastic + Novel ideology + High risk-taking appetite
Cons: Lack of maturity and experience + Lack of experience to avoid pitfalls.

30s to 40s: Passion + Experience: After Mark Zuckerberg made headlines, we developed a myth that a startup founder is supposed to be in the early to mid-20s to be successful. However, the median age for company founders when they started their businesses is 40. With age comes experience and maturity.

Moreover, you become more aware of the potential pitfalls. Any age group is a good time to launch your business ideas as far as approach and decisions are concerned. For example, Falguni Nayar worked with Kotak Mahindra for 18 years before starting Nykaa.

Pros: Experience + Access to more startup funds + bigger professional network

Cons: Low risk-taking attitude + Family responsibilities take priority

The 50s: Fully Experienced: Studies have shown that middle-aged business founders are two to three times more likely to succeed than those under the age of 30. Although a few famed tech entrepreneurs like Steve Jobs of Apple, Mark Zuckerberg of Facebook (now Meta), Bill Gates of Microsoft, and Larry Page and Sergey Brin of Google launched their companies in their 20s in the USA, age criteria became a little confusing. Even in India, Ritesh Aggarwal started OYO in his 17th year. However, many successful businesses were started by entrepreneurs in their 40s. Thus, do not let your age stop you. According to OnStartups, the median age of company founders when they started their current companies is 40. Contrary to the mythical tales of college dropouts, some 95 percent of 549 company founders surveyed graduated from college, and nearly half of them held an advanced degree.

Starting Business At Middle Age

According to a study from Northwestern University, USA, businesses tend to be more successful in the tech industry when started by those in their middle age. The study concluded that the most lucrative tech companies had a founder with a medium age of 45. The high success rate is attributed to the founders' experience. They have already made mistakes in their careers and potentially learned to avoid common pitfalls. In addition, older founders may have access to more startup funds and have a larger professional network. Moreover, middle-aged entrepreneurs are comfortable in the market and can spot gaps to fill.

ENTREPRENEURSHIP EPIDEMIC

When people contend that middle-aged people lack innovative ideas, I happily point out that Steve Jobs made Apple richer after he crossed the age of 45 and made the iPhone, iMac, iPad, and iPod. Sanjeev Bhikhchandani worked in several organizations before launching Naukri.com with his friend from a small room. The idea was to make an online database for resumes, and now we know how Naukri.com has revolutionized the way we look for jobs.

There is no age limit for business. As long as your idea is good and you are passionate to pursue it, you are fit to start your business.

A Dire Need Of Field Experience

"Success comes from experience and experience comes from bad experiences."
- Sandeep Maheshwari

As a problem strikes our life, we work hard to find a solution, and in this process of finding, we may succeed in some and fail in some. Those failures are often the more significant teachers than the successes. I am not against education; however, I feel the sooner one applies the knowledge gained, the better is one's chance to succeed. I emphasize field experience for the following reasons:

> **Applied Knowledge**: With a graduate degree, one can gain all types of theoretical knowledge, but is that knowledge useful if not applied at the right place at the right time? If someone really wants to do business in life, field experience can teach more practical and applied knowledge.
> **Differentiator**: The work you have done in the past and the projects you have undertaken are particular to you alone. A relevant experience makes you stand out from the rest of the people in the rat race, even if you choose to opt for formal education at a later stage in your life. We live in a world that is constantly looking out for uniqueness, something that differentiates you from others.

With field experience, you can craft your own story while the rest of the world remains glued to an old and obsolete script.

- ➤ **Self-Awareness**: Awareness of your strengths and weaknesses is the key to finding success. The most valuable contribution of field experience is self-awareness. Working on an actual job gives you the advantage of learning about your strengths and weaknesses and the areas for improvement and gives you an insight into where your passion lies. A hands-on experience enables you to identify whether you are fit for the job or not. For example, you might be a graduate of IIM, but without field experience, you may not really understand what you lack. Field experience is a must if you are lost while searching for your passion.

- ➤ **Soft Skills**: Employers want people to have realistic expectations about their jobs. Experience helps you learn about the everyday realities of working life and, most importantly, equips you with the soft skills needed to succeed at any organization. You improve your communication skills, learn how to manage a team, understand the importance of timely delegation, and develop the qualities of a leader. After all, if you are willing to start your own company, you should have the qualities of a leader. Developing such soft skills shall help you while you grow your business in the long run.

- ➤ **Networking**: While a college degree might increase your peer base, field experience gives you access to a huge network of people who have been there in the market longer than you. You get the golden opportunity to tap into their knowledge and learn from their mistakes. As your network grows, your practical knowledge widens, and you mature quickly to learn the pitfalls. Field experience is the best guide for your career planning.

Problems Are Actually Helpful

As I said earlier, problems prevail in every situation, and one just needs to attempt to look through them and provide a suitable solution. Let us understand the setting with Zomato's example.

Case Study: Zomato Success Story

Deepinder Goyal and Pankaj Chaddah, two alumni of IIT Delhi, were working at Bain & Co. in New Delhi. They would find themselves and others waiting for a long time to have a glimpse of the menu card. Once they got the menu card in hand, they were too bored to look for the variety of options and would end up buying whatever came to their mind from the previous purchase. The duo conceived the idea of developing Foodiebay after realizing this looming problem. They uploaded the soft copies of the menu cards on a website, and thereafter, everyone in the office utilized this provision to choose the food they wanted. It saved time, and people liked this facility. They expanded their website to make it available to everyone as they saw the idea succeeding. Foodiebay was initially started in Delhi, and then its services were extended to cities like Mumbai and Kolkata.

Foodiebay acquired huge popularity by rendering distinct services to the customers. This enabled the founders to scale the project to an international level. Soon the name was changed to **Zomato.** It sounded cool, bewitching, and eliminated any confusion between the website and eBay. Thus in 2010, Foodiebay was officially renamed Zomato. The usage of Zomato saw such a phenomenal upsurge that the founders decided to simplify the access to the application. A mobile app was developed to make Zomato easy to access. However, innovation demanded more funds.

The founder of the notable job search engine Naukri.com, Sanjeev Bikhchandani, was truly fascinated by Zomato's idea of delivering foods, and he invested in the project. In 2010, he invested up to US $1 million through Info Edge India.

And the next year the same investors provided them with a huge fund of US $3.5 million. The potential of Zomato was well-noticed as it showed the dawn of enjoying your favorite restaurants' food from the comfort of where you were. Another huge amount of US $10 million flooded in from Info Edge, which now holds more than 50 percent of the stake. Zomato got other financiers too. Sequoia Capital, Vy Capital, and Temasek, Singapore, invested their funds in Zomato. In October 2018, Zomato raised $250 million from the Chinese company Alibaba, and additional funds of around $150 million were raised from Ant Financial. Today when you sit at home and want to eat something in a relaxed mood, Zomato is the first name that comes to mind. You can order your favorite food from your favorite restaurant within a minute. In addition, the mobile app also provides you with the option of searching for different restaurants based on the cuisine you desire.

Today, after 13 years since its inception, the food delivery app has released its IPO, hoping to raise Rs 9,375 crore. Isn't this a big step? From witnessing the problem in an office canteen to becoming a prominent name in the market of food delivery, Zomato has come a long way. And the credit goes to the idea of two passionate people who could see a problem that no one else could.

Success Mantra: According to Deepinder Goyal and Pankaj Chaddah, hiring the correct persons remained the primary reason for Zomato's startling growth. It was not easy to find the right people at the right time. Essentially Zomato is an application whose business model encircles the provision of food delivery services, information, user reviews, and menus of partner restaurants. Zomato stands as the pioneer for other online food-based applications. It acts as the bridge between customers and partner restaurants, and it has crafted a well-designed pricing model for its delivery services. The inclusion of Zomato Gold and Piggybank has improved the quality of services provided by Zomato.

Growth: Zomato has partnered with various big names like Uber Taxi, Visa, and PayPal which helped Zomato in setting up its service at different locations.

Apart from handling Zomato's hiring process and market research, these partners have been taking care of the political and legal issues.

Challenges: The most significant hurdle they faced was finding a way to cover all the areas in all the pivotal cities so the people who hinge on them do not miss the finest restaurants. This remains a challenge even today, but the founders and the whole Zomato team endeavor to improve the situation.

Zomato's Business Model: During the initial days, the focus was not much on earning money. When the website attained huge acclaim, they recognized the prospects associated with it. Presently, Zomato has 62.5 million registered customers. And every other restaurant has now placed advertisements through which it can get huge revenues. Secondly, Zomato made it easier and safer by launching cashless transactions. It had a miraculous effect during the Covid-19 pandemic.

What do we learn? If one has an idea to solve an existing problem, one can always find funding sources to start the business. A great idea combined with a passion for bringing about a change is all you need to begin your journey in the business world. The success story of Zomato shows that hard work and determination will lead to achieving your goals. Ups and downs are a part of starting a business. We need to have a positive mindset and work our way to the top. Zomato's success story is not built on one pillar. The founders created a business model that played its part in building the brand of Zomato.

Why is Zomato loved? Zomato is immensely loved for the way it works. It is premised on the QAAA model, i.e., it promises and delivers Quality, Accessibility, Affordability, and Assortment to its customers and partners. Hyperpure is an innovative initiative by Zomato to bring fresh, clean, and high-quality ingredients and kitchen supplies to its partner restaurants. The success of Zomato Gold speaks volumes about Zomato's efficiency in providing an array of exciting choices. It has continually strived and left no stone unturned in delivering the best.

They present the best information in the most legible manner for their customers and help them make an informed choice.

How does an innovative idea help in the long run? The coronavirus pandemic accelerated the adoption of services offered by Zomato. The revenue from operations grew from Rs 466 crore in FY18 to Rs 2,604 crore in FY20, signifying around 5.5X growth over the three years. For the nine months that ended on December 31, 2020, revenue from operations stood at Rs 1,301 crore. The sole reason behind this success was the founders' ability to foresee the issue and develop an innovative idea. Even in times of crisis, Zomato thrived because its business model focuses on the delivery of essentials. As Deepinder Goyal says, *"Everything is solvable. You just have to put your mind on it."*

Doing Business Is Challenging

No business grows overnight. Business is not like walking on a bed of roses. Although I advocate the advantages of doing business or creating a startup, I would like to remind people of the perils that come along with the perks. Beware! One must work a minimum of 1000 days without expecting good results. Business is not a cakewalk and requires 24/7 commitment. Some of the major challenges are as follows:

- Choosing the right line of business and conceiving a better business strategy.
- You must inculcate the habit of patience. You must work for at least 1000 days without expecting a profit.
- Effective financial management and maintaining a regular cash flow are important to keep the business running. Remember! You are an employer now.
- You must hire the right talent and maintain a solid management information system (MIS). No business can grow without the right workforce.

- Effective time management. You are a human, and you cannot work 24/7 without balancing your work life with personal obligations.
- Delegating tasks. Why? Because you cannot do everything even though the business idea is yours. Effective people management is key to a successful business. One must acquire the right people for the right job.
- Proper Marketing Strategy. It is the 21st century, and the market is flooded with similar items. A good idea can become popular and acceptable once it is marketed well. There are umpteen modes to market your business, and one must know which modes suit one's business.
- Capital or Fund Raising. No matter how rich you are, you will need some helping hands to widen your scope of business. However, you have to find the right investor who understands your business strategies.
- Balancing perfection with progress is a little difficult but not impossible.
- Business Growth must be foreseen. The market is fickle, and the demands are ever-changing and ever-growing. Keeping up with the changing business scenario, market demands, technological advancements, marketing strategy, etc., will be challenging.
- Cultivating Humility. It is quite natural to develop some ego as you are your own boss. But remember, no man can be an island. You need to cultivate good relationships with your customers, investors, stakeholders, and employees. Humility always beautifies success.
- Planning ahead. A product that suits today may become obsolete tomorrow. Forethought is imperative for any business plan to succeed. It is not an easy job to plan ahead. Nobody had imagined Covid to cause such a big disruption in the business world. On the same note, companies that diversified quickly could survive the wave.

➤ Self-doubt. Though I mention this as the last, self-doubt is one of the biggest challenges faced by many in their business careers. Your abilities are not defined by your profit margin. As I said, it will take time for your efforts to bear fruit.

Key Takeaways:

➤ Starting a business is the best option in the current job market.
➤ Skill in sales is the key essential requirement to start a business.
➤ Field experience is more important than a higher educational degree.

So, Fear Not! Start your own business. Hone your entrepreneurship skills and be your own boss.

2

WHO DARES, WINS!

"If you don't build your dreams, someone else will hire you to help them build theirs."
— Dhirubhai Ambani

India has come a long way, laying the stones of success one by one in building the cobbled streets of a developing nation. A nation is never built by the politicians but by the common citizens who dare to change the prevailing situation. The business empires of present-day India were once startups. Today, Reliance Industries is one of the few who represent the growth and development of our country, and the Ambani family runs it. However, Dhirubhai Ambani was not born with a silver spoon. His father was a mere school teacher, and he grew up with modest means.

At 17, he migrated to Aden and started as a clerk at A Besse & Co. In the 1950s, it was the largest transcontinental trading firm east of Suez. He learned trading, accounting, and other business skills in due course of time. In 1958 Ambani returned to India, settled in Bombay, and began trading in spices. He named his nascent business Reliance Commercial Corporation.

He soon expanded into other commodities and followed a strategy of offering higher-quality products while taking smaller profits as compared to his competitors. His business grew quickly, and soon he diversified. Ambani turned his attention to synthetic textiles. He engaged with a policy of backward integration and diversification and gradually shaped Reliance into a petrochemical giant and later added plastics and power generation to the company's businesses.

I shall quote Dhirubhai Ambani here: *Think Big. Think Fast. Think Ahead. Ideas are no one's monopoly.* The principle of doing business remains universal. One who dares, wins! As I mentioned in the earlier chapter, your ability to sell anything and everything on earth strengthens your prospect to pursue business. A curious mind is always an added benefit. Now, let me ask you again: are you overwhelmed by the uproar over startups? What if your family has an established business empire? Will you make a grave mistake by joining your family business? The answer is a resounding NO. Switching to business, whether traditional or startup, is never a mistake. Once you learn the tactics of the game, you can always hit your goal to make a profit.

This chapter will focus on the difference between traditional businesses and startups. How do they vary in their mode of action and their distinct ecosystems, and how do scalability and technology play a key role in helping startups grow and diversify?

Traditional Versus Startups: The Ideological Difference

Do you know that with more than 8,900 tech startups and over 89 unicorns (as recorded in early 2022), India continues to be the third-largest startup ecosystem in the world? Although we were slow to pick up the pace, India is now home to some of the most innovative startups across various domains ranging from Ed-tech to health-tech and enterprise to hospitality. Business is an economic activity that includes the regular exchange process of goods and services and involves risk and uncertainty.

ENTREPRENEURSHIP EPIDEMIC

Any business stands on the aim of meeting needs through the supply of goods and services to customers and their satisfaction. However, some specific characteristics differentiate a startup from a traditional business unit. Startups are mainly distinguished by the following:

- **Focus:** Burning problem within the society, industry, or humanity at large.
- **Business Model:** Highly Scalable.
- **Organization:** In the process of organizing or unorganized. Startups are the nascent form of a business.
- **Funding Source:** Seed funds, Angel investors, Venture funds, which can go further to IPOs
- **Role of Technology:** Pivotal. As the idea is novel and the wish is to reach the target audience faster, every startup is highly dependent on technology. Most startups are now app-based.

Most startups in India have roped in an idea from Western countries and modified the concept based on Indian needs. For example, Ola cabs. The concept is the same as Uber, and it is giving tough competition to Uber in the Indian market. While the traditional concept states that the only aim of the business is to make a profit through the production and marketing of products. Products can be of various types. They do not focus on any burning issues prevailing in the market. Simply put, they follow the legacy. There are different scopes for traditional business:

- Manufacturer
- Distributor
- Retailer
- Franchise
- Direct Selling Concept

According to the traditional concept, the main objective is to maximize profit from material goods, services, ideas or information.

According to the traditional concept of doing business, any human activity directed toward acquiring wealth or earning a profit through the production or exchange of goods has been treated as a business.

Startups: Making A Difference

The startup concept is ever-growing and diversifying. As their prime focus is on a problem, the focal point of their business sticks to **Consumer Satisfaction.** The startup mentality states that a business earns profit through customer satisfaction. No business can ever grow or earn profit without satisfying its customers. Even if you are running a small grocery shop in your locality, your customers matter. They are not only the source of your earnings but also standard and permanent marketing agents for your business. Remember, word of mouth is the biggest publicity for any business.

The startup concept is about developing long-term relationships with customers. Earning profits must accompany a social responsibility. There is an aim to take care of a burning problem of the society and common citizens who are the potential customers. On the same note, the business ideology must work within the scope of the law. You cannot wake up and begin a startup manufacturing a drug banned in India. The concept is to make profits while maintaining social accountability. Startups are the modern businesses that see business as a socio-economic institution that is always responsible to society.

Let me describe the story of Ola cabs in India to clear any foggy thoughts about startups and how they make a difference. Bhavish Aggarwal is the founder of Ola, and Ankit Bhati is the cofounder who handles the technological facets of the company. Ola was founded in the year 2010 in Mumbai. By 2014, Ola had grown to a network of 200,000 vehicles across 100 urban communities in the nation.

Ola has become a commanding power in the Indian market, accepting more than 150,000 bookings every day. So, who should be credited for this grand success?

The idea, the hard work of the staff, or the paying customers? The answer is **Idea**. Half of your hard work is paid off once you get an idea to target a burning issue in society. If the idea is fruitful and profit-worthy, you will not have to wait long to gather resources to make it a profitable business.

Bhavish Aggarwal was left in the middle of the road while traveling to Bandipur from Bangalore. The driver left him in the middle of nowhere as he was unwilling to negotiate the amount. A young man of merely 25 or 26 years was left alone on the road, just because the driver did not like the decided amount. We do not know if that inauspicious trip to Bandipur had caused Bhavish any loss; however, I am sure that the horrible experience helped him devise the idea of Ola cabs. This incident made him realize that it is very difficult to get a cab that offers fair services without proper contacts. Any common man can become a victim of the arrogance of the drivers and their overpriced services. He did acknowledge the problem, but he could not find a solution. At that time, he was running his business Ola trips, which offered touring packages. One day while marketing his travel packages, a customer asked him to arrange for vehicles. That very question lit the lamp in his mind. He realized that people needed better cab services and not destination guidance.

Ola has been adopted from the Spanish word, Hola, which means Hello. The idea was to make the cab service easy and gracious. No, the idea was not new. Uber was already ruling the western market with the same concept. Even in India, Meru Cabs, Carzonrent, and Zoomcar were major competitors to Ola cabs. They faced many hurdles while developing a user-friendly app, accumulating good drivers under Ola, and transforming the manual process of booking cabs to online booking. The number of satisfied customers grew over the years. Due to word-of-mouth appreciation, Ola cabs would get their first angel investor in Kunal Bahl, the cofounder and CEO of Snapdeal.

By the time Uber was trying to figure out the marketing strategy of Ola Cabs, Ola Cabs had garnered a huge market share in India.

As of early 2022, Ola Cabs operates in over 250 cities, whereas Uber operates in just 46 cities in India. I would call Bhavish Aggarwal a good forecaster. He realized quickly that the mindset was changing. Not many would buy a car for it is like having a pet. There are many added hassles like the maintenance costs of cars, the cost of hiring a driver, the fuel costs, the trouble of parking, paying the taxes on the vehicle, and, not to forget, the congestion and poor condition of our roads. Do you know only 36.49 percent of Indians own cars? Even I believe that no one would want to spend the majority of his time driving amidst snail-paced vehicular traffic in the future. Moreover, many sane minds will eventually prefer shared transport, like shared cabs and shared buses, considering the traffic congestion and the growing rate of air pollution.

Now, you may complain that such apps need high-speed internet all the time. Then I must tell you that Ola has employed a win-win strategy by developing another app called Ola Lite, which can function even at 2G internet speeds. So, tell me, isn't the idea worth pursuing? Bhavish Aggarwal is an IIT graduate, and his leaving of Microsoft to pursue his business did worry his parents initially. However, today, they must be proud parents of one of India's young entrepreneurs.

Problems are worthy as long as you work toward finding the solution.

Ideology	Traditional	Startups
Concept	Production and distribution of products for personal wealth generation	Focus on the burning problems and innovative business plan to combat.
Orientation	Profit oriented	Customer needs and satisfaction.
Origin	Usually family-run business	Personal experience with the concerned problem

Assumption	Everything cheap is sellable.	Quality is the prime objective.
Ownership	Family run, Partners	Angel investors, Cofounders
Geographical Scope	Localized	Widened reach by technological intervention
Mode of Operation	Traditional mainly through cash transactions.	Heavily influenced by payment apps.

So, which one do I support? As a serial entrepreneur, I support the core idea of doing business, focusing on diversification. Change is inevitable, and we all should move ahead with the change. Forecasting is one of the key ingredients needed for diversification. Even if you are bound within the limits of a family-run business, you can always look out to spread your wings. If you cannot spot any viable opportunity, you can improvise on the payment modes. Many small-scale traditional businesses escaped the pitfall of demonetization by installing Paytm and other digital methods of payment.

The outlook toward startups may vary; however, the idea of pursuing business as a career must not waver.

Startups Turning Problems Into Opportunities

We must understand that sustaining profits is neither permanent nor secure in the present scenario. Technology is constantly evolving, which affects the products and services prevailing in the market. In terms of business, we call it the Product Lifecycle. With changing technology, the product lifecycle is becoming short; business models are changing, and new competitors keep entering the market. When entrepreneurs decide to launch their own startup, most of them go through similar important phases.

The first step for them is to develop a feasible and scalable idea. **Without scalability, there is no hope.** On the same note, some entrepreneurs will have ideas running through their heads for years (for example, Ola cabs) before actually implementing them. And then, there are others who have selling skills, financial backup, and resources to start but lack an innovative idea to distinguish themselves in the market. Ideas, feasibility, and implementation strategy play a crucial role in either case. Even the best of the ideas shall turn useless if not implemented.

The feature that distinguishes an ordinary idea from an extraordinary one is the possibility of transforming it into a saleable product or service. Consequently, we must understand that not all ideas are opportunities. Most startup ideas emerge due to the following reasons:

- *Internal Reasons:* The entrepreneurs start looking in the market for opportunities and needs that they can meet by offering a certain product or service.
- *External Reasons:* The entrepreneur notices the **gap** in the customer needs and sets forth a new startup idea.

An opportunity should have several specific qualities, such as the right timing, the right product, or an added value that the service offers to consumers to encourage them to purchase it. There are three key points to consider before planning your new business.

1. *Seek The Opportunity To Grow*

The year Narendra Modi turned India's transactional finances upside down, a new trend of digital payment took birth. Vijay Shekhar Sharma, the founder of Paytm, has crafted an original story of rags-to-riches. Demonetization served as a blessing in disguise for Paytm as common people and small-scale businesses that were legion of our country looked to Paytm to sustain their lives. Before demonetization, Paytm had 125 million customers.

Three months after demonetization, the number of customers grew to 185 million. By 2017, they had 280 million users. As they say, darkness is needed to see the stars. Paytm was an idea that changed how the common Indian thought of doing financial transactions. Vijay Shekhar observed the growing phenomenal use of smartphones. He wanted to contribute to society so that people could use smartphones to transact online. On July 8, 2010, an online website called Paytm.com was launched under its parent company One97 Communications. Initially, it served only from online prepaid mobile and online DTH facilities. Within a couple of days, it was popularized among people due to its facility of paying the electricity, water, and gas bills. Paytm made people's life easier. Within two years, the number of its users increased to 250,000. Paytm had become a popular name in the world of e-commerce.

Two words that come to almost every Indian's mind while shopping post-demonetization are "*Paytm karo.*" Paytm has brought about a paradigm shift in the retail industry by completely transforming the payment methodology. This online wallet cum e-commerce website was initially used to make payments for limited utilities like mobile and DTH recharge and shopping bills. Over the years, this portal has expanded its scope and has brought almost everything under the ambit of its operations. Customers now can recharge their metro card, pay bills for utilities like electricity and water, transfer funds to other bank accounts, book flight/train/bus tickets, make hotel reservations, etc.

Now the latest Paytm Success Story is ever-expanding with the addition of e-retail and m-commerce stores. Paytm has given the option to small vendors to list their products on its website and allows them to expand their customer base. The Reserve Bank of India has approved the Paytm e-wallet, i.e., the user's money is secured under the escrow account with a nationalized bank. The security feature and easy user interface make Paytm the most favored digital payment platform in India. This online payment system is not only safe but also robust. One of Paytm's success stories is that it can handle around 5000 transactions per second.

A high volume of transactions has been made possible by a very easy yet efficient and secure payment method. Users can simply pay by either scanning a QR code of the shop or by entering the mobile number of the recipient. The Paytm wallet also has a choice where users can safely park their money in the application and pay via the app. Paytm is driven to improve its products and services and strengthen the customer experience. Their committed team energetically works to enhance a single characteristic no matter how tiny it may be. Paytm has proven to be an ideal in the run of e-commerce software developers, and its huge rise in craze has motivated others to follow it.

2. *Solve The Problem*

We all know Falguni Nayar as the Beauty Entrepreneur of our country. Age can never be a hindrance to solving an existing problem. The cosmetics market in India has been inconsistent, to say the least. Even though the market demand was high, India's beauty and cosmetic products and market were not on par with those in countries like France and Japan when it came to scope and quality. Additionally, the products were also unavailable in many places around the country. These problems seemed like a glorious opportunity for Falguni Nayar, and Nykaa was born. Founded in 2012, it initially started as an online corporation and eventually switched to an omnichannel strategy.

Nykaa's mantra is to make every simple woman extraordinary in every aspect. And as Falguni Nayar often quotes, *"Retail is all about Detail."* Nykaa is a D2C consumer products e-commerce brand that relies on an inventory-based business model. The company purchases its products directly from the manufacturers and keeps them in its designated warehouses located in New Delhi, Mumbai, and Bangalore. These products are sold either on the website of Nykaa or through its three offline store formats: Nykaa Luxe, Nykaa On Trend, and Nykaa Kiosks. The inventory-led model of business of the company helps the company witness high-profit margins.

It has also resulted in a profitable business. Besides, the company also ensures the authenticity of products and follows competitive pricing. Nykaa reported Rs 2,440.89 crore of revenue generated in FY2021, which surged around 38.10 percent from what it was in FY2020. Nykaa earns its revenues through the sale of products and banner advertisements. The banner advertisements of the company also help bring in a lot of traffic, many of which turn into sales.

Discount income, income from commissions, and miscellaneous income are other revenue sources for the brand. Nykaa claims to have 15 million registered users with more than 70 stores across India. The company boasts the availability of 500 brands and 130,000 high-quality products through its website, app, and physical stores. The unicorn cosmetics and beauty products brand has witnessed a major shift of the consumers toward the essential categories, including personal skin and hair care items. This change helped Nykaa expand faster than its rivals after the COVID-19 ambush. Furthermore, the company's shift from an online model to an omnichannel retail model also contributed a major part to its expansion. Customers changed their perception of the brand, and Nykaa could gain audiences it could not target earlier. Nykaa successfully launched its IPO on October 28, 2021. It has already turned into a public company limited by shares on July 16, 2021, and had filed its Draft Red Herring Prospectus (DRHP) back in August 2021.

The valuation of Nykaa surged almost to $13 billion on its Indian market debut. Nykaa's parent, FSN E-Commerce, witnessed a record rise in its share values on the stock market on November 10, 2021, which resulted in 96 percent returns on the investments of the company's investors.

3. Bridge The Gaps

As soon as one starts earning, the first step is to insure against the contingencies and emergencies of life. Insurance policies help manage risk and cash flow uncertainty and are good investment.

It used to be very common that agents who sold insurance failed to provide options that could cover the customers completely. They knowingly or unknowingly hid crucial policy-related information from gullible individuals. The agents often sold irrelevant policies solely for their benefit and commission rather than prioritizing the customer's requirements. Previously, the insurance industry was opaque and convoluted. Honestly, a big chunk of the client's funds went into fattening the agent's wallet. Over the years, customers developed an aversion toward the agents. Yashish Dahiya founded PolicyBazaar in 2008 to bring transparency and accountability to the Indian insurance policy segment. PolicyBazaar turned unicorn on June 26, 2018, becoming the second Indian unicorn.

The company initially compared the prices of insurance policies and provided insurance-related information. The company saw rapid growth and has further expanded on many horizons. Along with being an insurance marketplace, the company further extends assistance for the cancellation/renewal of policies and settling claims. It provides life insurance, health insurance, motor insurance, travel insurance, group insurance, etc., and offers more than 250 insurance plans and around 50 insurance brands on its platform. The platform is designed so that the visitors can easily compare insurance plans and buy the ones relevant to their needs.

Through PolicyBazaar's 'My Account' feature, customers can easily download a policy, raise a ticket, ask for clarification, and upgrade policies. PolicyBazaar also introduced a self-inspection video feature to revive lapsed motor insurance. The company has adopted Amazon Polly and developed PBee, an in-house AI chatbot, to improve customer satisfaction. Yashish Dahiya is an investor and the founder of paisabazaar.com, which provides fixed deposits and loans at your fingertips.

An incident of insurance misselling sowed the idea of PolicyBazaar in Yashish Dahiya. PolicyBazaar works on building a safety net for households in India. It enables common Indians to make informed choices while making policy selections.

The company has partnered with insurance brokers to procure information, such as price, benefit, and insurance cover for customers to compare. Based on the information provided, the customer then chooses the best option. It does not charge customers anything for this service. Consequently, PolicyBazaar makes money by generating leads for insurers, advertising, and policy sales. Till 2011, 85 percent of its revenue came from lead generation and advertising, while the rest came from policy sales. However, by 2021 85 percent of the revenue comes from e-commerce and policy sales.

Let me give you some tips to ponder while choosing a business opportunity:

- Listen to the market. Observe the customers. Find out the shortage.
- Do you find a competition for your idea? If yes, how do you wish to make your idea stand out from the crowd?
- Keep an eye on the industry trends and insights. You must know the flow. Remember, going against the tide needs a lot of effort and knowledge.
- A change begins at home. Think like a common man. It is always useful to solve the problems at the grassroots level rather than thinking of building a life on Mars.

Potential Area Of Business

It is true that the one who dares, wins. However, a bold step in business must come along with an effective execution policy. Any business proposal must be conceived after foreseeing the probability of its survival. We call it a SWOT analysis in terms of organizational policy, i.e., analysis of strengths, weaknesses, opportunities, and threats. In this section, let me enlighten you with some of the major sectors that have shown a better prospect in the changing market.

FINTECH (Financial Technology): The banking sector is probably the most untapped market in India because most of the Indian population does not have a bank account.

Fintech startups are thus gearing up to make a difference. Many noteworthy fintech companies have brought much-needed disruption and innovation to this conservative sector in the last few years. The ruling government's enthusiasm to make India a cashless economy resulted in a plethora of cashless payment technologies such as internet banking, mobile-driven POS, and digital wallets. In turn, the financial sector has been restructured. Seeing the prospects of a fintech company, it has become the most preferred investment choice for venture capitalists and individual investors for quite some time now. With the entry of global players like Google, Amazon, Uber, and PayPal, India's fintech sector is all set to experience a massive revolution, especially when it comes to digital payments.

Health Tech (Healthcare Technology)

Quality healthcare must be accessible to all, and accessibility is still a major challenge in most parts of India. Technological advancements have expanded at lightning speed in the last decade. Although rural areas are in need of a major change, a majority of the hospitals, doctors, and pharmacies still prefer urban areas to set up their operations.

Health-tech startups are a promising business idea in this scenario. In the last few years, many health-tech companies have tried to bridge this gap by making healthcare services accessible to all parts of the country. Today's health-tech entrepreneurs are thinking beyond traditional healthcare services like diagnostics, medicine delivery, and enterprise. New health-tech startups are more focused on solving prevailing healthcare issues and addressing the root cause of health issues with the help of technology. The solutions may lie in timely diagnosis, reducing mental stress, recognizing and preventing genetic disorders, improving consumer lifestyle, etc.

With the help of cutting-edge technologies, health-tech startups ensure easy accessibility to up-to-date medical records, history of genetic disorders, and lifestyle choices for effective and timely treatment.

Some startups in this space are Practo, Healthkart, 1mg, DoctorInsta, Lybrate, Pharmeasy, and Zoctr.

Logistics: India's logistics startups are mainly driven because of the keen interest shown by foreign investors. The new startups in this sector have increasingly focused on implementing new and innovative technologies to create better and more effective solutions that can fix the existing flaws in the supply chain. For example, data collection and real-time tracking have been made more efficient with the help of the Internet of Things (IoT).

Additionally, machine learning and artificial intelligence are now increasingly used for route optimization. In 2019 alone, many Indian startups like Paytm, Ola, FirstCry, Delhivery, and Grofers have been on a rollercoaster ride of mergers and acquisitions. Disruptive and innovative ideas emerged as the real winners, and startup funding reached record levels. The Indian startup ecosystem has witnessed an unusual trend over the past couple of years. Although the total number of deals has gradually fallen, the deal value has reached some exorbitant levels. Investors have invested a large amount of money, but only in fewer well-established startups. Let me tell you here that those mentioned above were the major Indian startups that attracted some valuable investments.

Enterprise Technology: The one thing that makes businesses in India more efficient, productive, and profitable is enterprise technology. It has introduced them to ERP management and SaaS technologies. Numerous small and medium enterprises have successfully leveraged SaaS and other advanced techniques to optimize their processes. Some of the leading startups in this space are Freshworks and ZOHO. Inventory management and accounting startups have also made significant advancements in the last couple of years.

Consumer Services: Food and grocery delivery services have been among the hottest startup sectors in India.

Food delivery unicorn Zomato has generated a whopping $206 million in revenues for the FY2018-19. And Zomato has now acquired UberEats in India. At the same time, Swiggy is giving tough competition to Zomato. The biggest names in grocery delivery are Big Basket and Grofers, to name a few. As I see, they all made hay during the tough phase of the pandemic and lockdown and raised the bar.

EdTech (Education Technology): Let me tell you very frankly; education is one sector that can never run into a loss. EdTech companies have grown in leaps and bounds during this tricky COVID period. Schools and colleges have not functioned properly, and many students had to go online and embrace the virtual classroom using technology. Due to this, the demand for online learning modes has also grown tremendously. There is an extended emphasis on technology-driven education systems further with the New Education Policy, introducing students to coding. If I have to quote the recent report, India's EdTech market might reach a value of $3.5 billion by the year 2022. This includes the estimation that Class 1 to Class 12 will create a valuation of about $1.7 billion, and post-class 12 will create about $1.8 billion.

In the Edtech sector, one startup doing really well is BYJU'S. It has enjoyed significant growth in the past few years. The lockdown attracted a lot of new customers to their website. In April 2020, the company earned around Rs 350 crore.

Byju's also acquired another EdTech company called WhiteHat Jr., which provides coding classes to school students foreseeing the advantage of the New Education policy. The Byju's app blends three main attributes—content, media, and technology—to deliver comprehensive, highly appealing learning material. Byju's makes great use of data science to provide customized learning experiences. Interestingly, the company can personalize the learning instructions through its "Exhaustive Learning Graphics" technique: once the platform successfully establishes a learner's style, the app can recommend videos and activities accordingly.

Byju's enjoyed a monopoly before the COVID-19 pandemic. However, many similar major players entered the market when the government-imposed lockdowns and limited physical attendance in schools and colleges. The tough times paved the way for other EdTech companies like Vedantu, Unacademy, Toppr, and Meritnation.

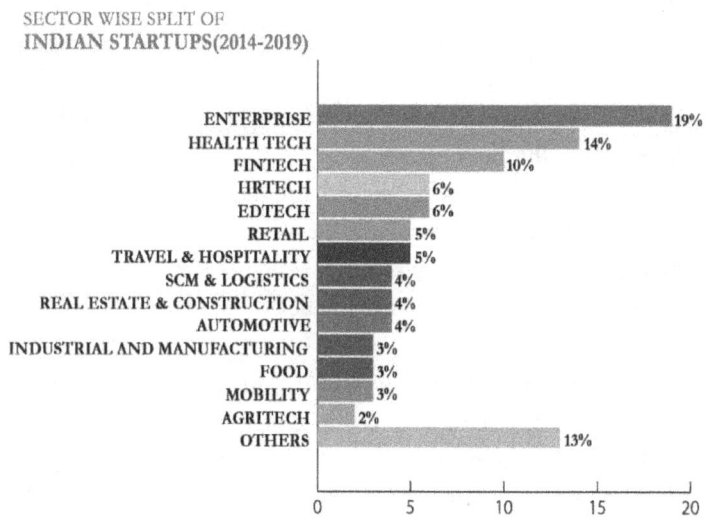

Which Business Model Suits You?

Understanding the problem your business proposal seeks to solve for your customers is the biggest challenge while starting a business. Ensuring that your product/service fits the market's needs is only one part of starting a successful business. The other vital segment is about making money out of your business.

A business model elaborates how a business organization creates, delivers, and captures value. Whether you carry forward your traditional family business or become an entrepreneur, your business model must work through nine building blocks:

Types of Customers, Value Propositions, Channels of Doing Business, Customer Relationships, Modes of Revenue Generation, Key Resources, Key Activities, Partnerships, and Cost Structure. Let us have a brief overview of different business models:

- Low-Volume, High-Margin
- High-Volume, High-Margin
- Low-Volume, Low-Margin
- High-Volume, Low-Margin

There is no universal rule for choosing a business model. No single model is the best or the worst; each model works best in a particular set of industries. In general, the models exist by default. It is highly improbable that you can move your small business into another one of the types without changing the particular business sector or the industry. Let us take a quick look at each model.

Low Volume - High Margin: As the name suggests, building the final product is time-consuming. Moreover, the selling price must cover the operational cost, facilities cost, human resources, cost of licensing, and profit. Large companies that follow this model are mainly involved in these sectors:
- Aircraft manufacturing – Boeing
- Heavy Equipment manufacturing – Caterpillar, Komatsu, Hitachi & Volvo
- Military Equipment manufacturing
- Large Industrial/Commercial Contractors – Bechtel, Fluor & Kiewit
- Heavy Transportation – shipping lines, railways

There are small businesses in Engineering Design/Build Companies, Metal Fabrication, Marine Fabrication/Construction, and Home Construction/Remodelers/Renovators. We can see that in this model, although it is a low-volume company, the term reflects the physical quantity and not the currency value.

For example, the construction of ONE aircraft reflects less production volume, but the amount is expensive. Certain business attributes that force the industry to exercise this model are as follows:
- Significant initial capitalization (financially, perseverance, knowledge).
- Almost all work is project-based and requires extended periods to complete.
- Highly complex interactions and resource management.
- Little competition.

High Volume – High Margin: This model is the most preferred type of business model; however, these types of companies are not very common and often have significant capital barriers to starting operations. Mostly they are in the professional services industry such as law, accounting, engineering, and some medical specialties. In general, the margins are in the 40 percent to 50 percent range. This is mostly attributable to variable costs as the primary cost.

A few examples of these types of businesses:
- Coffee Retail/Coffee Supply
- Software Manufacturing
- Entertainment (Music Albums, Movies, Videos, Games)
- Hospitality Based Businesses (Hotels, Motels, Golf Courses, etc.)

This type of business model is ideal as the overhead and capitalization costs are higher than in other models. Competition is intense as others seek to enter this type of business model for the same high margins this model provides. Another factor that nurtures the high-margin requirements relates to higher-than-normal fixed costs.

Low Volume – Low Margin: It is the most interesting of all the business models. Why? Do you doubt its profit-making ability?

I shall tell you another way to look at the equation. Less experienced business entrepreneurs always think of margin in terms of percentage of sales. Experience and a little more sophistication teach us that it is really about absolute money. Let me ask you a basic question here: what would you prefer? Sale of 100 units per day with a 15 percent margin or the sale of only 1 unit with a 12 percent margin? It depends on the selling price. Selling 100 units with a selling price of Rs 10/unit will fetch you a margin of Rs 150 while selling one unit with a selling price of Rs 5000 will bring you a margin of Rs 600. Usually, our household goods and high-ticket items follow this model:

- Auto Retail
- RV Dealerships
- Marine Dealerships
- Appliance Sales
- Jewelry and Luxury Goods Retail.

One of the negative attributes of this model is the higher-than-normal risk associated with acquiring customers. Any reduction in market share can wreak havoc with the financial profitability of the business.

High Volume – Low Margin: It is a business model traditionally seen in retail and other consumer-based product businesses.

- Convenience Stores
- Petrol Bunks
- Grocery Stores
- Fast Food Restaurants
- Retail Outlets
- Transportation (Bus Lines, Distribution, Taxis, etc.)
- Service-based operations in more discretionary income-dependent areas of business
- Nail/Hair Salons, Massage Parlors

This model has the low capitalization threshold to enter.

It is the most common form of business in our consumer-based society. This reflects several business attributes:
- Easy entry for small business
- Low capitalization barriers
- Low knowledge thresholds
- Many support systems
- Reduced government compliance requirements
- The gross margin is a direct reflection of volume. Competition is significantly intense in this model.

As you can see, each of the models described above works for particular industries. The sheer nature of the industry forces their hand into the respective model. Now tell me, when you think about your business proposal, which model is the best for you?

"Ideas are cheap and abundant; what is of value is the effective placement of those ideas into situations that develop into action."
— Peter Drucker

Are You A Good Salesperson?

There is no point in becoming an average salesperson if the success of your business depends on your skill in sales. Going the extra mile and becoming a good salesperson is far more important for customers than an exciting pitch. Be enthusiastic with resilience and take time to know the customers' needs. Show empathy, and deal in a product with confidence. You must understand that success will not run behind you. There will be rejections, and you should know how to handle one. *Build your success slowly; learn from your mistakes quickly*. Let me give you some tips to become a good salesperson.

- **Identify and stick to your buyer personas.** Remember! You cannot sell computers to a person looking for a good restaurant to eat at.

- **Use a measurable, repeatable sales process.** Keep a watch on your selling tactics. Is it making a profit?
- **Know your product.** You cannot sell a sanitary napkin if you do not know what it is all about.
- **Review your pipeline objectively.** Make accurate forecasts. Do not overestimate your capacity.
- **Practice active listening.** Speak less and listen more. The market has more experienced people than you. Learn from their mistakes.
- **Work hard.** Business is not for lazy people. Ambanis are not made in dreams. They work hard in the real world.
- **Follow up.** Nobody is perfect. Always follow up with your customers to understand the loopholes.
- **Personalize your message.** Your business must display the essence of humanity. Do not preach but nurture a demand for your product.
- **Shadow your peers.** Your competitors are your best teachers.
- **Practice your people skills.** Your product is inanimate, but customers are not—communication skills matter.
- **Be a team player.** No man is an island. You need people from different backgrounds to give you overall growth.
- **Know when to walk away.** Every business comes to a halt. Know when to diversify.
- **Be honest.** Honesty is always the best policy.
- **Stay balanced and take breaks.**
- **Do you know your strongest motivator?** Unless you are motivated to do business, you cannot sell anything.
- **Are you thinking ahead?** Come out of the rat race. The world needs people to think out of the box.
- **Your potential customers are everywhere. Look for them.**

The Sales Techniques

We have to understand that the present generation of customers is more educated than ever and has many options available to them. They DO NOT compromise on quality anymore. As we know, modern sales techniques revolve around the art of communication while structuring a mutual benefit for the business and the customers.

So, what do you need to become successful in sales? The answer is simple—deliberate and persistent activities and the ability to simultaneously adapt to market changes and services. Selling is a science with rules and regulations that have been thoroughly analyzed and researched over the years. There is no universal method that fits all scenarios. Every business demands its own mode of selling. Let us have a close look at the different selling techniques.

➤ Cold Calling

This technique is about making calls to unknown prospects. The idea of cold calling sometimes seems scary to some business owners. However, one must remember that one's company offers a solution to a problem. That realization can make your effort seem less daunting. In my opinion, one should ask questions or seek suggestions regarding the customers' needs or challenges instead of telling the prospective customer about your product. Listening skills play a vital role in this method. One must identify the existing problems first before you recommend your company's solutions.

➤ Seek Referrals

This is a traditional sales tactic where a business creates a campaign to seek referrals from its satisfied customers. The process works in two ways. You can ask customers if they know anyone who would need your company's products and services or request them to share your contact information with other prospective customers.

You can also initiate a call to the referred prospect.

The second tactic requires identifying people who know your customer and with whom you would like to form a business relationship. You can then ask your existing client to introduce the person to strengthen your hold.

➤ Direct Mail

In this process, one can identify the prospects through an effective sales letter, accompanied by a reply mechanism that indicates the prospect's interest. This traditional sales model is especially helpful when one does not prefer to make cold calls but wishes to find new prospects you would not be able to reach otherwise. The process starts with obtaining a mailing list consisting of the names and addresses of your target market. Once the recipients read your direct mail letter, they send back the enclosed reply card to express their interest in obtaining more information. You must continue to send periodic newsletters or additional marketing mailings to convince your prospects to buy your product or services to convert them into paying customers.

Direct Mail is still one of the easiest ways to reach the decision-makers. Marketing research has proven that consumers, traditional or digital, still find the mail a relevant and efficient source of product information.

➤ Print Advertising

Print advertising is often called the cave art of the 20th century as the concept took birth a long time ago. However, it was more pronounced after the Industrial Revolution during the mid-1700s. The times have changed now, and advertising methods have taken a vibrant facade to display their promotional discount or new products. Print advertising often pushes people to websites and social media sites for more information. Rates vary from a few hundred rupees for local publications to more than lakhs for bigger coverage in national magazines or newspapers with a higher circulation. The key to success lies in running the ad numerous times. One cannot expect profits from a single ad.

Print advertising knocks at a prospective customer's doorstep and gives a visual impact. While reading through newspapers or magazines, prospects get to know about your brand, products, and availability. As Daniel Starch said, *"The simplest definition of advertising, and one that will probably meet the test of critical examination, is that advertising is selling in print.* Business psychology substantiates the fact that a visual impact is always stronger to convert a prospect into a paying customer.

➢ Signage Advertising

Signage is a broad term that includes any graphical representations or displays whose objective is to convey information or a message to an audience. Signage advertising is a model to advertise or promote a brand or business with a graphical display. Signage materials comprise digital photos framed and lighted in the dark. We are thriving in the world of digitization. With advanced graphic designing techniques, signage advertising has walked out of dull walls to mobile taxis, thus reaching a wider audience than ever before.

From sidewalk signs to roll-up banners, window graphics, pylon signs, signage advertising is like vintage wine that could never lose its charm. Signage advertising gives high customer exposure and can create brand awareness 24/7. On the same note, visibility and space constraints do pose a problem.

➢ Billboard Advertising

Billboards are typically placed in high traffic areas, such as along highways and in the cities' business hub, which bear the highest number of drivers and pedestrians. It is effective for building brand awareness and broadcasting your business.

Billboards using printed or hand-painted images on canvas are still very commonly used. Billboards have come a long way from highways to hallways, using less text and more peculiar images to grab attention. Larger signs can never be overlooked, and billboards can never turn obsolete, given their wide reach across social classes and geographical boundaries. Billboard advertising is often called OOH-advertising, as they promote a product to the customers when they are 'out of their homes.' The cost involved depends on several factors, including your billboard's location, the total traffic in the area, and how many people are estimated to see your advertisement.

Billboard advertising designs range from Tell A Short Story to Make It Bold or Make It Interactive based on the board's location. The key to success lies in how memorable is your advert. I would say peculiarity sells faster than soberness.

> **Flyers and Brochures**

There lies an immense power in word-of-mouth advertising and handing out methods. Brick and mortar establishments, street corners, or malls are places where any new or existing business can distribute flyers and brochures. Even in the age of social media, this remains the most widely preferred method for special discounts and offers. How can we undervalue the concept of business cards that directly introduce a business to the client? By connecting to prospective customers face-to-face, traditional marketing is way more interactive and effective. Handouts can bring any business new growth opportunities. Direct mail and business cards often elicit emotional reactions and are more closely absorbed than words on a screen. Flyers often evoke strong responses and greater reach for marketers.

> **Face-to-Face Interaction**

Real-time physical meetings trump virtual meetings any day, anytime. Face-to-face promotion of any product is the most conventional mode of marketing. Traditional marketing methods from signage to networking at events, cold calls, and referrals take advantage of the power of human interaction. If you want to close a sale, go for face-to-face interaction; nothing is better than that.

Tangible, physical canvas, paper, and traditional marketing mediums evoke a sensation and a lasting memory. These are also easier to retrieve than logging onto a visual storefront or a digital calling card online. Effective and honest communication skill is the essence of such an advertising method.

➤ Event Marketing

Event marketing includes the process of developing a themed exhibit, display, or presentation to promote a product, service, or organization influencing an in-person engagement. A business house can conduct events online or offline, which can be participated in, hosted, or sponsored as a form of engagement. Organizing events gives the potential customers a unique, firsthand interaction with the company and a true sense of the company's focus, perspective, products, and personality. As I said earlier, today's buyers are educated and self-directed about making purchasing decisions. They are careful in their consideration, so marketers must be ready to seize every opportunity to start a relationship, generate goodwill, and earn the trust of prospective buyers. The conventional way of copyright marketing is a story of bygone days; now, it is all about generating a buzz.

Event marketing has brought in a novelty in face-to-face interactions and customer networking. Though the recent trend is about SEO marketing or Social Media marketing, event marketing has got its own pull. Apart from helping in building brand presence before, during, and after the event, one can generate leads, add on value, and find new opportunities. Event marketing often helps promote a specific product or feature and increase overall customer satisfaction, retention, and engagement. Planning events can also give your partners and sponsors a tactical and visible engagement point to enforce their own return on investment. A buyer's journey is 70 percent complete before even the salesperson directly contacts the customer. Sales and Marketing is an art that one must inculcate through effective communication, appealing demeanor, and product/service knowledge. Salespersons act as the catalyst in the process of marketing. Sales skill is needed in both online as well as in offline marketing. A good salesperson develops his knack with time and experience.

> *"Sales are contingent upon the attitude of the salesman—not the attitude of the prospect."* - W Clement Stone

Customer care and customer retention play a vital role in converting prospects to solid customers or even acquiring new customers. The core value a sale generates is an excellent product or service. Remember that no amount of good marketing can ever sell a bad product, and without effective marketing, even the best of products fails. Marketing is an art that derives its value from traditional techniques because this is the way it has always been done. Traditional marketing covers wide demographical sectors from baby boomers to Gen-X, Gen-Y, and millennials to the swaying sixties. While digital marketing continues to gain ground, traditional marketing techniques remain an important secret weapon for interactive, face-to-face, and skilled marketing.

Challenges In Traditional and Small-Scale Businesses

The present business world is ultra-competitive, thanks to the advancement of technology and the involvement of the digital world. Let us look at the major challenges faced by traditional or small-scale businesses.

Lack of Ample Funding: Money is an essential requirement for running a business. Cash flow or money management is a difficult and nerve-racking challenge faced by every small business owner.

The current economic situation has made everyone run in a marathon race within the scope of cutthroat competition. Most businesses start with a limited amount of money and, in the turmoil of the beginning years, the hardest challenge is to maintain regularity in the cash flow. At the birth of a business, the invested money returns mainly from the payments received. When the savings are almost empty, it becomes difficult to fill the gap with payment retardation. Unplanned expenditures often occur in the changing scenario of the market. The lack of ample funding at the right moment often hinders a small-scale business.

Chalking Out The Correct Marketing Plan: Marketing challenges are another evil giant that 76 percent of small businesses fight. Digital marketing and online resources have changed the entire landscape of marketing strategies. Buyers have all sorts of resources for gaining knowledge, and it is harder to convince the customers than ever before. And amidst all the competition, it becomes difficult to chalk out the most profitable marketing strategy. For example, a small-scale grocery wholesaler cannot opt for billboard advertising. One must plan according to the target audience and budget. Some of the key considerations are as follows:

- Create a profile list for your target market.
- Try to be wherever your potential clients can be found.
- Choose proper media platforms. Create an account on well-known professional sites.
- Keep your content brief and precise. If you opt for digital marketing, DO NOT forget the SEO optimization tools.
- Stay connected with your customers 24/7.
- Provide analyzed records about your work.
- Research your market ambiance and create your own niche.
- Show feedback from your existing clients.
- Never ignore negative reviews. Always respond and seek suggestions to rectify the issue.
- Create your app to be accessed from any device.

It is also important to maintain a complete picture of your marketing and sales records. You need some marketing and sales tools to keep up with the modern technological trends. However, you need to focus on the critical aspects of budget estimation and distribution before looking at the tools. Critically observe your ROI calculation. Manage your responsive website with load time optimization and security.

Targeting And Retaining Customers: In this era of digitization, modern business is centered on customer orientation. Online marketing and resources have educated your customers on almost everything. But there is still something you can do to show your unique features by enhancing your customer service system. One can use social and professional channels to reach their target clients. Try to connect with them through personalized service channels, such as email, and chat sessions. Find out their needs and briefly explain how you can meet them. One must express one's creativity. Customers always judge your expertise within your niche, so be prepared with relevant information. Never make customers wait for long. Provide free demo services. Carefully create offers that direct your customers straight to the solutions they need. Deliver analytical records and customer feedback whenever required. It is hard to convince a new customer to close a deal, and 78 percent of them leave before purchase due to unsatisfactory customer service.

Remember, your existing customers are the directors of your success. Their feedback and comments are the most reliable source of information on your reputation for new customers. Apart from this, the chances of persuading an existing customer to purchase are 60 percent to 70 percent, whereas it is only 5 percent to 20 percent with a new one. Research your existing customer database and sales records. Decide which ones are your best customers. Also, focus on negative feedback and learn what you need to do to resolve the issue. Compare satisfied and unsatisfied customer records and find out the reasons for your success and failure.

Strategic leadership: Have you read the book Leadership Unleashed by Thomas Norofsky? There is a wonderful statement about effective leaders in that book. *We need leaders who can meet and adapt new challenges, build strategic partnerships, build human organizations and have the courage to act and react to the challenges. Leaders are the pioneers of the entire team, and the success of a team depends on the qualities of its leader.* A true leader can see the whole picture of the business, including customer and employee behaviors. A leader must search for new updates and relevant information sources to plan a profitable strategy. Learn from experience. Connect with other experts and ask for their opinion.

If you wish to lead your team to success, make sure you have a firm grip on these abilities:

- **Listen to everyone.** It is the most significant quality that differentiates you from the rest. You need to listen to other leaders and experts to grab valuable ideas. Listen to your employees to create a productive work culture. Listen to your customers to understand the market demand.
- **Motivate your employees.** A good leader must have a clear vision and mission for the company and encourage everyone toward a successful accomplishment of tasks. Let them know about every little achievement they accomplish. Train them well to avoid past mistakes and encourage them to open up about their confusion and feedback. Gain their trust; sympathize with their problems and create a communicative environment around the entire team.
- **Be knowledgeable**. Educate yourself first before preaching to others. You have to be the master in your field in every way possible. Be open to options for new ideas. Research all the analytics that you get.
- **Learn from your mistakes**. Do not be afraid to fail. Everyone is bound to commit mistakes; however, one must learn not to repeat the mistakes.

The business world is cruel, and you cannot escape from its wrath if you keep repeating your mistakes.

- **Dearth of talent.** This is a big issue that every small business or traditional businesses face. Do not be directed by emergencies and salary issues. Seek out the right person for the job. Do not mix the talent pool. You cannot be a jack of all trades. Not every salesman is capable of planning marketing strategies. Similarly, customer service staff can never handle your sales work. You must decide well on the job profile before hiring the right person. Upgradation is the need of the hour, so train your existing employees regularly. Demonstrate solutions to their mistakes and provide lessons on new technologies. Encourage them with experience-based studies. Hire job seekers with the proper experience. Even a well-qualified individual can hinder productivity if placed in the wrong place at the wrong time.

***

I always had the vision to make a business go beyond its boundaries. With my uncle as an angel investor, I started my own company Meridian Infotech Ltd. to grasp a share in the IT business. I did not wish to sail on two boats simultaneously and thus handed over the Wipro business to my partner. It was a great leap for me due to my company becoming a business partner with IBM for their AS/400 Enterprise Platform and ERP Software on the national market. I would press on the sales skills that acted as the catalyst. In addition to the new business of ERP and AS/400 Platform, I also started a separate division in Meridian for the upcoming sector of IT Infrastructure for Networking. Success was not handed to me on the very first day. I had to wait for 1000 days to succeed, and my patience and perseverance paved my path to success. However, did I always succeed with no blot of failure? No. Never

#

> *My first failure popped its head with my decision to go with IBM AS/400 Platform. The IT sector was going through a major overhaul at that time, and Microsoft was focusing on the Enterprise platform of Windows NT and related products.*
>
> *So, I started to sell ERP in the Microsoft Platform and cultivated a good clientele in India and Africa using Reckoner ERP from Ascomp Technologies Pvt. Ltd., New Delhi. As I could include IT Infrastructure as another vertical, it further helped Meridian Infotech Ltd. to become a formidable player in the Indian market as we were the preferred partner of Cisco in various segments of the industry. I am proud to tell you that in FY2021-22, Meridian Infotech Ltd. has entered the Rs 100 crore turnover club for the first time, which has been one of the major contributions from my cofounder and partner Devang Jasani.*

Key Takeaways:

- Learn the ideological difference between traditional businesses and startups before you start.
- Tricks to transform a problem into an opportunity.
- Learn about the potential areas to start your business and the most suitable business model.
- Learn the different techniques to sell.

Individually, we are just a drop, but we can build an empire together. I believe you have understood the scopes of doing business—problem to solve, business idea, target audience. But then, can you start all alone, or do you need a partner?

3

PARTNERING THE RIGHT WAY

The basics of business are written over the principle of togetherness where different ideas are encouraged to bloom.

What if I tell you that it is mutual trust that plays the strongest role in building an encouraging and cohesive environment for any business to prosper? You could be someone born with a silver spoon who has rightfully inherited a big business empire. However, all said and done, 'No man is an island.' No matter how bright your ideas are or how efficient a leader you have been, you are bound to feel saturated at some point in time. This saturation can come in the form of a knowledge gap, technical deficiency, or financial constraint, or it can be any situation where you are in dire need of guidance or a helping hand.

"It is rare to find a business partner who is selfless. If you are lucky, it happens once in a lifetime."
— Michael Eisner

Considering the concept of partnership, it is not restricted to the business world. We are social beings and are bound to develop human relationships at different stages of life. We hatch the notion of partnership right from our childhood, with our siblings.

Soon cousins, and friends join in. All dealings in life, whether personal or professional, work out only within a cohesive environment. The design of a partnership is simple; however, the execution of an effective partnership is complicated.

Why Do You Need Partners In Business?

Here, I shall begin with Ratan Tata's famous line: *"If you want to walk fast, walk alone. But, if you want to walk far, walk together."* Every business runs on multiple tracks simultaneously; thus, it becomes essential and also beneficial to have different minds and different skills coming together.

A partnership is a crucial ingredient for the growth of any business venture, and let me tell you this, the idea of developing partnerships has been there from time immemorial. Merchants and traders used to employ the principle of a strategic partnership to conduct their businesses.

A partnership establishes itself in different forms, such as business owners cooperating to invest in a project to share technical knowledge and ideas between firms or when an established business owner discovers the hidden opportunity in a small-scale business and invests in it financially. There are various components in a business partnership; nevertheless, I should emphasize a very critical aspect here. An efficient partnership is built on the foundation of mutual trust and shared passion. The principle of partnership is dissolved if one of the partners is losing his meal while the other is minting money. You have to remember that your business is much like your blood and soul and you must nurture it to grow and prosper further. Running a business is never a stagnant process and you must choose a partner who will approach your business with the same level of enthusiasm and commitment and also shares the same business parenting philosophies. A partnership is a long-term, legal agreement between two (or more) people. And before you choose a partner for your business, let us have a quick look at the benefits of having partners in business.

- **Widening of Knowledge:** Investment in knowledge gives the best returns, come what may. Different partners bring in their skills and knowledge onto a common platform and such strategic partnerships always enhance the knowledge of the whole team. Partnerships give an opportunity to grow by learning a different perspective. Gaining knowledge and skills that are better and more refined can enhance a brand or a business.

- **You Get a Competitive Advantage:** When we talk about traditional businesses, there remains a void for innovation. For example, if you are running a dealership business in computer parts, you will face tremendous competition in the market. Partnerships not only help increase your knowledge and expertise but also provide better resources to build better products and reach a wider audience.

- **Enhanced Business Credibility:** The right business partnership always enhances the culture of your company. Partners indeed share the same goals and vision and their joint effort influences and strengthens each segment of the organization. Stronger businesses provide better products and deliver more qualitative services to customers, which boosts the overall brand equity.

- **Stability:** Every business has one philosophy in common—to remain relevant for a longer time and reach the desired and destined corporate goals. Relevance comes with adjusting and adapting to the changing needs and market demands. Having business partners means you are no longer operating in isolation in a market that is always volatile. Your business acquires more stability as you possess enhanced knowledge, innovation skills, diverse expertise, and funds. A great business partnership makes your business better.

It rectifies your weaknesses and improves your strengths, and imparts everything you need to keep your business relevant for a long time.

➢ **Increase in Customer Base:** Many business partnerships run on functional strategic partnership agreements. This helps your business to grow its customer base. Certain partnerships work on a direct agreement to offer products that are complementary to your own. For example, a car manufacturer can enter into a partnership agreement with a tire manufacturer, whereby each customer of the car manufacturer automatically becomes a customer of the tire manufacturer company as well. Or if you are running a business of interior decoration, you can make a partnership agreement with a renowned real estate company.

➢ **Division of Labor:** As your business grows, the organizational hierarchy changes in structure too. Gradually, your business would demand specific and specialized divisions for General Management, Sales, Marketing, Distribution, Operations, Human Resources, Law, and Finance. It cannot be a one-man army if you wish to survive. Different partners handle different departments based on their expertise.

"Seek out strategic alliances; they are essential to growth and provide resistance to bigger competition."
— Richard Branson

Partnerships In Family Business

A business partnership is a way of organizing a company that is owned and sometimes run by two or more people or entities. It is a legal relationship that is most often formed by a written agreement between two or more individuals or companies.

The partners invest their money in the business and each partner benefits from any profits and sustains part of any losses. As traditional businesses often run down a family line, the concept of partnership begins right at the threshold of the home. Every business, whether traditional or a startup begins from a point with a founder. As the generations progress, the reigns of the business are transferred to the next generation. In case the next generation has more than one inheritor, different segments of the same business are handed over to the different inheritors. There are many family-run businesses where brothers/siblings, cousins, or close relatives entered into a partnership to let the business diversify and grow.

There are many family-run traditional businesses that have diversified and grown and made their prominence felt in the Stock Exchange. Let me brief you on some of the major family-run businesses here.

- ➢ **Reliance Group**: The beginning can be modest, but the aspiration must be like a mammoth. Dhirubhai Ambani started a yarn trading business from a small 500 square feet office in Masjid Bunder, Mumbai, but dreamed of establishing India's largest company. Reliance set up a mill in Naroda, Gujarat, sparking off Reliance's backward integration journey. Mukesh Ambani led the establishment of Reliance's first mega manufacturing project at Patalganga in a record 18 months. Gradually, the company moved into petrochemicals, retail, mobile communications, bioscience research, and financial services. The founder of Reliance Industries, Dhirubhai Ambani, died in 2002 without leaving a clear succession plan. The different sectors of the business were then divided between his two sons, Mukesh Ambani and Anil Ambani.
- ➢ **Godrej Group**: Founded by Ardeshir Godrej and Pirojsha Godrej in 1897, Godrej is one of the major family-run multinational conglomerates in India. Ardeshir Godrej started a surgical equipment manufacturing business.

It all started with a loan of Rs 3000 from a family friend, Merwanjee Cama. The surgical equipment manufactured was of exceptional quality and Godrej had printed the words 'Made in India' on them. The instruments were exported to England. Though the British approved the quality, they did not like that 'Made in India' stamp. The business of surgical instruments failed as Godrej was too patriotic to abandon the tagline. While observing the felonies in the neighborhood, he decided to start a business in Locks. And the rest is glorious history. Presently, the company has products ranging from hair dyes to furniture, CCTVs, chemicals, air conditioners, and real estate. From toiletries to broiler feed, the Godrej family business is ruling across the borders. Adi Godrej is the Chairman of the Godrej Group. Nadir Godrej leads the Godrej Agrovet sector and Nisaba Godrej handles the consumer products. Tanya Dubash manages the brand and chairs Nature's Basket

- **Mahindra Group**: Mahindra & Mahindra was incorporated as Muhammad & Mahindra in 1945 by the two brothers J. C. Mahindra and K. C. Mahindra, and Malik Ghulam Muhammad in Ludhiana, Punjab, to trade in steel. After partition, Ghulam Muhammad left for Pakistan and the Mahindra group became an exclusive family business. Presently, the company has been completely professionalized and Anand Mahindra serves as Emeritus Board Member.

- **Bajaj Group**: Founded by Jamnalal Bajaj, the Bajaj group showcases an epitome of business legacy. Kamalnayan Bajaj finished his education from Cambridge and joined his family business and diversified it into the manufacture of scooters, three-wheelers, cement, and electricals and alloy casting. The present generation includes Rajiv and Sanjiv Bajaj after demise of Rahul Bajaj. Presently, the company has diversified into automobiles, financial services, home appliances, electrical goods, sports, and even insurance.

- **TVS Group**: The company was founded by T.V. Sundaram Iyengar and is now having numerous subsidiaries held under three major holding companies of TVS & Sons, Sundaram Industries Private Ltd., and Southern Roadways Private Limited. Venu Srinivasan and Suresh Krishna, the present Chairmen, are TVS Iyengar's grandsons.
- **Munjals Hero Group**: Brijmohan Lall Munjal was the founder of India's biggest motorcycle maker, Hero MotoCorp. The family business was originally started by three brothers in 1944 and dealt with bicycle parts. Om Prakash Munjal started Hero cycles in 1956 with a bank loan of Rs 50,000. From manufacturing bicycles, they moved into mopeds, and then motorcycles after entering a partnership with Honda Motor in 1984. The partnership went on to become the world's largest motorcycle producer. In the late 1990s, Om Prakash became one of the first to explore the idea of manufacturing electric bicycles in India. In 2010, the family split 4 ways, with Brijmohan's faction taking over control of the Honda JV. In the same year, Om Prakash assumed responsibility for leading Hero Cycles, Hero Motors, Munjal Kiriu Industries, ZF Hero, and Munjal Hospitality. In 2011, the Munjals ended their partnership with Honda. Brijmohan Lall's eldest son, Pawan, chairs and runs Hero Motocorp now. Om Prakash, his brother Brijmohan, and the next generation of the family were instrumental in establishing Hero Honda, which is now Hero Motocorp. Eventually, they have encroached in the electric vehicle sector with Hero Electric.
- **Jindals**: The Jindal family embarked on their business journey way back in 1952. The first venture of the Group, Jindal India Ltd., was set up in Howrah, West Bengal, as a manufacturer of Mild Steel, ERW, and Black Galvanized steel pipes/tubes. The Jindals are the first and foremost manufacturers of steel pipes and tubes in India.

They are also the first to set up a fully indigenously designed pipe and tube plant in India. After establishing a lead and consolidating their position in steel pipes/tubes, they diversified into tea plantations in 1980. The Jindal group went into manufacturing Partially Oriented Polyester Filament Yarn (PFY) in 1985, Casing Pipes in 1987, Photofilm in 1987, Off-Shore Oil Drilling in 1989, and Seamless Pipes in 1992. Talking of their beginnings, Bhavi Chand Jindal, the second oldest son of Netramji and Chandrawali Devi Jindal, planned to go East, following the astute advice of his father. His brother Devi Sahay accompanied him as the Jindals set their eyes on Calcutta and Tinsukia, Assam. These destinations seemed to offer better prospects for advancement when compared with those present in the simple rural environment of Nalwa, their native village. It was somewhere between 1945 and 1946 that they started working as trainees in the wholesale cloth trade as well as in retail textile merchandising. Through their ingenuity and innovation, the family business diversified into different avenues. Presently, Sajjan Jindal and his brothers, Prithviraj, Ratan, and Naveen, each manage their own businesses that were primarily inherited from their father.

➢ **Arvind group:** They began their business in 1897 when Lalbhai Dalpatbhai set up his first mill called Saraspur Manufacturing Company. The year 1931 witnessed the family's involvement in the Swadeshi Andolan when the Lalbhai family started Arvind Mills, creating a capacity to compete with the world's finest textile mills. After two decades of success in the textile industry, Kasturbhai Lalbhai set up India's first dye and chemical plant, under the aegis of Atul Products Ltd., and reduced India's dependence on imported dyes and chemicals. Arvind Mill's Flying Machine was India's first denim apparel brand, which was launched to meet the aspirations of the emerging youth.

Through tie-ups with V.F. Corporation (USA) and Cluett Peabody & Co. USA, for manufacturing and marketing, Arvind was able to offer high-quality global apparel brands like Lee Jeans and Arrow Shirts to the Indian market. Sanjaybhai Lalbhai is the current Chairman and Managing Director of the Arvind and Lalbhai Group, and his son, Punit Lalbhai, leads Arvind Advanced Materials, Engineering, and Agribusinesses.

Organizational research has proven that family-owned businesses account for two-thirds of businesses worldwide and they play a vital role in both economic growth and job creation. On the same note, although family businesses are major economic drivers, only a mere 30 percent of them are carried forward into the second generation, 12 percent last into the third generation, and just 3 percent make it to the fourth generation. All the aforementioned family businesses are still running successfully as they follow some of the following precepts:

They have defied convention and have made open, regular communication an essential part of the family business. Every business is bound to have conflicts. Effective conflict management ensures the longevity of the business. The key mantra is to Evolve. Check the evolution tree of any of the successful family businesses. They would all have started with something small; however, they slowly and steadily grasped the changing demands of the market and diversified their business. Many family businesses failed because of their aversion to new technology or resistance to changing cultural norms. Evolution and diversification are essential for sustenance.

Leaders of flourishing family-owned businesses know that setting boundaries is critical to establishing and maintaining success. Institute and uphold a clear separation between family and business. Family conflicts must not be reflected in the board rooms. All the successful family-run businesses ensure that they have their bloodlines chairing the top positions, although they always hire external brains for better governance.

They all have a professional, advisory, or supervisory board comprised of non-family members with a limited number of family representatives. Successful family companies tap into the external talent pool for skills and expertise family members do not have. They treat employees like family. If you do not consider this feature as significant enough for success, then I would suggest that you talk to the employees of TATA, Reliance, etc. A business grows with better employees and better employees are retained with good treatment.

Proper succession planning paves the path to longevity. Successful family businesses do not just let the chips fall where they may. They plan for the future, creating family business succession plans long before they actually need them. Ensuring an efficient partnership between the family members is the key to success, where each member is designated with a specific scope of the diversified business.

Choosing The Best Partners

> *"If your business partners are not working as hard as you, it's not a partnership. It's a sinking ship."*
> – Julian Hall

These are some of the key features to look for while choosing the best partner for your business.

- ➢ **Shared Passion:** Look for a business partner who can help take your company to the next level as that is the crucial step for the success of any business. Find a partner who has a shared vision for the organization and strives to move the business forward toward the same long-term goals. Equally, it is important that you share similar values, entrepreneurial spirit, and working styles, and have compatibility with a potential business partner. Remember, even the greatest of business ideas can easily be damaged by a negative business relationship.

- **Straightforward Communicator:** A good business partner is always direct. I often say that what goes on inside your head is always hidden from the world. People can never read your mind unless you voice your plans. You have to tell people what is on your mind in a direct, straightforward manner. Nothing is truer in business. Sometimes your ideas will be fruitful and sometimes they can be utterly terrible. A business partner who is straightforward can bring honest feedback to any situation. Every business is better when partners are direct with one another.

- **Skilled In Your Field:** I suggest looking for potential business partners who have a firm understanding of the industry. Always look for people with experience, education, and references, and also preferably, a personal brand website. When you connect with someone with these traits, you will have more time to focus on improving the business from within. As an added bonus, partnering with another expert in the industry can boost brand awareness.

- **Ethical:** Having the same work ethic is a key ingredient to finding a successful partnership in my experience. It is hard to notice this trait unless the partners were former co-workers or had worked together in any capacity with you previously. Most of the time, people are enthusiastic when it comes to starting a business, but then they realize how much work is involved day-to-day and fade out or slow down. This could frustrate the other partners or start various conflicts. When they have the same work ethics, partners would have the same priorities and easily agree on almost everything, which makes running a business smoother. In other words, efficient partners form a successful business. Your core values should be discussed early on and understood, so when rough waters arrive, you will have the confidence in your partner.

- **Balanced Strength and Resourcefulness:** You can be intellectually connected with a person, you can have complementary skills, you may hail from a different or the same background, and you may have so many more connectors that traditionally speak for a good business partnership. The one thing that you cannot buy and is not easy to find is stamina. Stamina comes into play when things get tough, which are usually the moments when you need your business partner the most. In these moments, there will always be a push-and-pull relationship between two business partners. This is healthy and helps to get through tough times. However, if that determination, strength, and resourcefulness to get through tough times is not balanced, then it is hard for the partnership to survive the stress.

- **Diversified Business Skills:** Diversified business skills are critical when selecting a business partner. The partner should have the ability to take on different tasks within their separate skill sets and cover the core competencies of the business. You will need to dig a bit deeper and truly understand that all parties must have the same set of business and personal values, nevertheless, with their own diversified roles. Aligning your values is critical because your business will inevitably send you countless challenges, and you will need to lean on your core values as a team to fight your way through.

- **Previous Success:** The most important thing to look for in a business partner is a complementary skill set, not an identical or similar one to what you already possess. The key to knowing what to look for is having an accurate and impartial understanding of your own strengths and weaknesses. Similarly, scrutinize the past experience and knowledge of the partner.

> **Growth-Addicted:** You really want to align yourself with someone who has a long-term vision in mind. If you partner with someone who is in it for quick success, they will be less likely to stick around when things do not go as planned. You need someone who is reliable. Someone who is looking five years down the road. Someone who is determined to find solutions to the many challenges and obstacles that can and will pop up along the way. Someone who is dedicated to your vision and purpose. For your business venture to be successful long-term, your partner needs to have the same level of dedication as you as well as a growth mindset.

When Friends Became Partners

All lasting business is built on friendship, so said Alfred A. Montapert, the famous American Philosopher. A partnership between friends happens when they find themselves nurturing a mutual interest and complementary skills. If a vision is shared between two friends and one of the two is skilled in technical knowledge and the other is good with marketing, the vision can be transformed into their business goal.

Let me give a few case studies of some of the successful businesses that began without a family heritage of doing business. Their success lay in their effective partnership and distinguished ideology.

Asian Paints: Painting India In The Colors of Success

In 1942, when thousands of Indians were writing a glorious chapter in India's freedom struggle through the civil disobedience movement, four friends in Bombay planned to begin a paint manufacturing company in a tiny garage. The British had banned the import of paints and that left the country with very limited options—either Shalimar Paints or other expensive foreign brands.

Champaklal Choksey, Chimanlal Choksi, Suryakant Dani, and Arvind Vakil decided to enter a less explored territory and translate their ambitions into reality with the 'Asian Oil and Paint Company Private Limited.' This company, with a random name that was derived from a telephone directory, is now almost 80 years old and has captured a 53 percent market share in India and is Asia's third-largest paint company. It is now known as Asian Paints and operates in 16 countries across the world. The company's marketing strategy kindled nostalgia with its 'Har Ghar Kuch Kehta Hai' tagline. The idea was to provide thousands of color shades, themes, textures, and patterns to its entire customer range, from middle-class households to corporates and even NGOs. There is a paint for every kind of budget.

There is an old-school thought that the success of a product is defined when there is no specific target audience, so that it caters to every type of individual. This strategy worked wonders for Asian Paints' massive popularity three years later in 1945. That year, the company invented tiny paint packets as opposed to giant tins to simplify and speed up the distribution process across the country. It established tie-ups with small distributors in every corner. In 1954, the paint giant decided to go all out and initiate a marketing campaign that would reflect its philosophy. This strategy was also a way to ensure that the existing customers remained loyal, and thus was born the notorious kid with a paint bucket and brush in his hand, Gattu. So, what was the outcome? The desi company could clock a revenue of Rs 3.5 lakh in the same year with just five color choices—black, white, red, blue, and yellow. This strategy helped them pick a steady pace and by 1952, the annual turnover of Asian Paints was Rs 23 crore, a sum that was considered to be huge back in the day.

Being consistent in quality but adapting to current market trends and developments is one of the biggest reasons for the company's exponential growth. Whether it was their first-ever TV commercial in 1984 or call-center operations and a website as early as 1998-99, Asian Paints has always stayed ahead of time by anticipating future trends.

The company has also not shied away from exploiting social media fervor and has millions of followers over Facebook, Twitter, and YouTube combined.

Infosys: The Breed of Engineer-Entrepreneurs

Infosys was conceived in 1981 in Pune by Narayan Murthy, Nandan Nilekani, NS Raghavan, S Gopalakrishnan, SD Shibulal, K Dinesh, and Ashok Arora. They are all former employees of Patni Computer Systems. Infosys Consultants was started with a meager initial capital of Rs 10,000 that Murthy had borrowed from his wife Sudha Murthy. Believe me when I tell you this—The front room of Murthy's home was the company's first office and the registered office was Raghavan's home. Infosys did not have a computer till 1983, because Murthy could not afford to bring an imported option he liked. It took almost two years to get a computer of their own. It was a Data General 32-bit MV8000.

Infosys faced a crisis in 1989 and one of the partners, Ashok Arora, quit. The others were undecided, while Murthy was firm enough to stick to the company. Nilekani, Gopalakrishnan, Shibulal, Dinesh, and Raghavan decided to stay and since then it has been always like that.

HCL Technologies: An Aspiration So Mammoth

The year was 1976. It was lunchtime at the Delhi Cloth Mills, popularly known as DCM. Six young engineers were discussing their work woes at DCM's calculator division in the office canteen. Their job paid them well and yet they were an unhappy lot who wanted to do more, riding on their own practicality. They decided to quit their jobs and start a venture of their own. The man who was instrumental in kindling this ambition within his other five colleagues was a 30-year-old engineer from Tamil Nadu, Shiv Nadar. And this is the story of how Hindustan Computers Limited (HCL) began. Nadar and his five colleagues quit DCM in the summer of 1976.

They decided to set up a company that would make personal computers. They had acquired the technical expertise at DCM's calculator division, but getting the necessary funds remained the problem. Nadar had to gather cash to give wings to his idea of manufacturing computers. He floated a company called Microcomp Limited through which he sold teledigital calculators. This venture threw up enough cash and enabled the founders to give shape to their ultimate dream of manufacturing computers in India, at a time when computers were just sophisticated cousins of the good old calculator. They also received support from the Uttar Pradesh government.

Finally, the founders put together Rs 20 lakh, and HCL was born. Ajai Chowdhry implanted the idea of computerization while expanding the company to Singapore. HCL provided hardware, software, and complete packaged solutions. Sensing the increasing demand for computer training, HCL set up NIIT in 1981 to impart high-quality Information Technology education in India.

Larsen & Toubro: The Danish Duo

The L&T story begins from before the Second World War. Two Danes arrived on Indian shores in 1934 and started this venture. Henning Holck-Larsen was a chemical engineer specializing in cement technology and Soren Kristian Toubro was a civil engineer. Soren Toubro arrived in 1934 to erect and commission the equipment supplied to Madukkarai Cement Works, near Coimbatore, and Rohri Cement Factory in Hyderabad (Sind). Henning Holck-Larsen came in connection with the merger of cement companies that were later grouped into the Associated Cement Companies (ACC). Both represented F.L. Smidth & Co. (FLS) of Copenhagen (Denmark) and had been friends since college days. When World War II began in 1938, they failed to return home as Denmark was occupied by Nazi Germany. They decided to stay on in India and with a little investment of their own, they joined Mr. Desai from Bombay to start a partnership firm.

A table and a chair in a small room—that was L&T's first office. Initially, the firm did not have much money. So, one person would sit in the office to maintain the accounts and make phone calls, while the other went around trying to drum up new business.

> *"Coming together is the beginning. Keeping together is progress. Working together is success."*
> – Henry Ford

Possible Scenarios Of Equity Sharing

Do not be afraid of the hefty term of Equity Sharing. It is just another name for shared ownership or co-ownership or a partnership in any business that has more than one owner. The sole purpose is to blend every skill and ideology to maximize profit and tax deductions.

- **One Finance – One Executioner:** In this kind of partnership, one partner is responsible for bringing in the funds while the other executes the business operations; the latter also brings in the exclusive knowledge of the industry. Profit sharing is straight 50–50 in this scenario.
- **Multiple Friends/Partners:** In this kind of partnership, profit sharing is based on the capital contribution and leadership role. One of the partners has to take up the leadership role and become the poster boy for the business.
- **Finance Partner – Working Partner:** In this kind of partnership, the working partner has no contribution in capital investment but brings his/her expertise in managing the business. Only 20 percent to 30 percent equity is shared and the working partner is provided monthly remuneration while working as a full-time employee. The finance partner on the other hand is responsible for infusing funds into the business.

> **Main Promoter with Employee Pool**: This is a unique scenario where the main promoter of the business enters into a partnership with the company's employees. Ion Exchange of India Limited is a good example of such equity sharing. With its patriarch retired and the majority of the employees holding the shares, the business has been sustainable to date.

Meridian Infotech Ltd.:

This is officially my first company where my uncle, Jayesh Buddhdev (Chartered Accountant), had invested as an Angel Investor, while I brought in some funds from my previous business with Wipro PCs. Meridian Infotech began with a 50–50 partnership. However, whenever funds fell short, I had to borrow funds at the market rate of interest. The initial 1000 days were tough but I had to be patient. A friend of mine worked with us and handled the other operations. As the business widened and Meridian became our major earning source, I gave one-third partnership of the company to my friend and moved on to develop other scopes of business. Later, my friend became the CEO of Meridian Infotech while I remained as an investor and my uncle as a mentor. Meridian Infotech Limited remains a good example to prove the significance of mutual trust and proper succession planning. Further details can be found at www.meridian.co.in

5 Point Solutions Pvt. Ltd:

This was my encroachment into the domain of ERP software while setting up the company with my cousin. Here, the business idea was mine while my cousin took the responsibility of execution—from production to end-user client. It is an equal partnership deal. Further details can be found at www.5pointsol.com

Excelsource International Pvt. Ltd:

Excelsource International Private Ltd. (EIPL) was established in 2004 and offers complete Sourcing Solutions to engineering goods, plants and machinery, consumable items, hospitality industry, and turnkey project management to our clients in the African countries. Here, I am the managing director and we are 3 partners with a pre-decided percentage of profit sharing. My brother-in-law is one of the partners in EIPL and thus, it exemplifies the concept of partnership amongst family members. Further details can be found at www.excelsource.co.in

Bright Agritrade LLP/BNSAgri:

Incorporated in 2019, it is a limited liability partnership. My cousin and I, along with two other friends started this company. While my friend and I are minority owners, my cousin and another professional are the majority holders. Each of us contributes the capital based on our prescribed sharing ratios. BNS Agri is our subsidiary, which handles the business in Singapore, Togo, and other West African countries. Further details can be found at www.bnsagri.com
#

Secrets To Sustain Partnerships

Business partnerships build an ocean of countless opportunities for your business to succeed and grow stronger. Starting a business with family or friends might look smooth as butter; however, there has never been any business in this world that has never faced a conflict of ideologies. Building partnerships helps in strengthening business opportunities in several domains. Having a partner is like never feeling alone in your pursuit of success. While there is a chain of legal processes involved while creating a business partnership, there is a dire need to sustain a strong and successful partnership. Business partnerships are similar to any other relationship: they require effort to maintain and must stay mutually beneficial.

And much like in a marriage, business partners too often have to swim through rough waters. Here are some of the questions that you must ask to ensure a long-term partnership.

> ➢ **Are you on the same page?**

Never jot down your business plan until you understand your partner's business goal and vision. The first question to ask is about the values one possesses to run the business. You and your partner must share the same core values, goals, and work ethic if you want the business to succeed. No business can succeed if one partner sees the business as a part-time occupation. All the partners must contribute toward the company's goal.

> ➢ **Is your business structure, right?**

You can organize a partnership as a general partnership, limited partnership, or limited liability partnership. However, you can also organize it as a Private Limited company or a Limited company. Each form of business has its advantages and disadvantages in terms of liability, taxes, and continuity. Before you enter into a legal agreement with your partners, seek advice from a company secretary and a legal advisor to determine which form of business would be the most suitable for you and your partner.

> ➢ **Do the partners have complementary skills?**

Only when you and your business partners have different strengths, can you double the power of your business team right off the bat. For example, an introverted computer genius can initiate a software business by entering into a partnership with a sales and marketing expert. Similarly, an apparel brand can diversify into the online domain of business provided they have partners who have prior experience with the same. However, an apparel business cannot run without someone skilled in the textile industry.

> **Have you demarcated the roles and responsibilities?**

There is a saying that too many cooks spoil the broth. However, in the world of business, every partner is like a different spice that comes with its unique feature and in turn, improves the final outcome. During the nascent stage of a business, each partner has to be a jack-of-all-trades to keep the business running. However, in the long term, each partner must have their roles and responsibilities clearly defined. Defining each partner's job title and duties helps eliminate disagreements by giving each partner control of his or her domain. Employees and customers also benefit from knowing which partner handles what aspects of the business.

> **Do you know the track record?**

A background check is crucial before roping in any new partners for the business. A person can be knowledgeable but a risk-averter, which is never good for a business. Look out for a partner's decision-making skills, temperament, social behavior, and team-management skills. Always remember, a business is run by a satisfied workforce. A financially strong partner who is ill-tempered may not be suitable for handling the Human Resource section.

> **Have you signed a legal document?**

Even if you are starting a business with your best friend from kindergarten, you must make every partnership legal by spelling out your business structure, capital contribution to the business, decision-making clauses, and resolution of disputes. Apart from these, there must be a clear mention of the clauses pertaining to leaving the partnership. Never consider legalization as a matter of doubt. It is just a mode to avoid any future conflict to sustain a long-term partnership.

> **Are you honest with each other?**

Strong, honest communication creates trust between both parties and helps set clear expectations while discussing all aspects of business strategy, such as financial concerns, dealing with errors and mistakes, and choosing the most suitable management style from a variety. Soft-pedalling your true feelings to avoid hurting your business partner will cause more problems than it eliminates. Sweeping your concerns under the rug will eventually only serve to aggravate the resentment, which is more than enough to ruin your business.

> ➤ **Are you proactive in conflict management?**

The business lifecycle is not only about unicorns and rainbows. Rough patches, misunderstandings, and disagreements are inevitable. If something is not working out, do not be afraid to offer suggestions and make improvements. Actively seek out new information that can help you build a stronger relationship. There are times when partners have to forego their personal benefits to let the business prosper well. Always find what works best for your partnership and find a good balance or middle ground between the two of you.

> ➤ **Give Respect – Earn Respect**

Partnerships work on mutual trust and pillars of friendship. Be real and transparent while dealing with your business partners. You need not agree on every issue but respect your partner's interests and opinions. A partnership is sustained only if both the partners feel secure in their roles and contribution. Never abandon new ideas without learning the proposed perspective.

> ➤ **Are you consistent?**

It is also important to maintain consistency and follow through with the promises that you have made in your agreement.

Nothing will end a partnership faster than not fulfilling the commitments that you have previously made. Be sure to check in regularly with your partner to know where you both are standing, whether that involves scheduling a meeting every so often or going to lunch and talking things through. Check in regularly to be consistent with one another and know that your goals are following through. Whether you choose to follow the traditional business model or wish to tread the path of entrepreneurship, partnering in the right way is an essential step to progress.

Conflict is unavoidable in business, which is a blend of success and failure, peace and chaos. You cannot master both but can chalk out a balance to let the business reach its goal.

Key Takeaways

- ➢ Understand the distinguished role of different partners.
- ➢ Features to check for effective partnership.
- ➢ Ways to manage/avoid conflict between the partners.
- ➢ Exploit the expertise and make Partners in Progress.

PART 2
STARTUP ESSENTIALS

4

STARTUP: WHO-WHAT-WHERE-HOW

Is your Google feed filled with news of the rising stars in the business world? Are your mornings spent stumbling over innovative ideas to start a business of your own and yet you have no clue where to begin? I am sure, the previous three chapters would have given you a fair idea of how starting a business can be a lucrative career in the present times. And if you are inundated with great ideas to set forth on your entrepreneurship journey, let us find out the who-what-where and how of inaugurating your business career. For many years, investors treated startups as small businesses, and there lay the real problem, because there is a huge conceptual and organizational difference between a startup, a small business, and a large corporation.

> *"Startup is a temporary organization designed to search for a repeatable and scalable business model, while the small business runs according to the fixed business model."*
> – Steve Blank

A startup founder's role mainly revolves around three main functions:

- Provide a vision of a product with a set of characteristics.
- Create a series of scenarios of the business model regarding customers, distributions, and finance of the company.
- Understand whether the model is the right one, based on customers' behavior, as your model predicts.

Thus, a startup is a company or business proposition designed by an entrepreneur to seek, develop, and validate a scalable business model. You have to understand here that there is a fine line to distinguish between entrepreneurship and startups. While entrepreneurship can remain unregistered, a startup always intends to grow beyond a single founder and diversify with the incorporation of technology. 'Startup' is the present buzzword around the world, and I am sure, you are all acquainted with the terms 'Unicorn' and 'Soonicorn.'

Understanding Startup

Startups are typically established by a founder or cofounders as a way to solve a problem. The business proposition starts market validation by identifying a problem and its probable solution. The next step is the building of a minimum viable product, i.e., a prototype with a specific business model in mind: B2B (Business to Business), B2C (Business to Customer), or D2C (Directly to Customer). And, as stated earlier, a startup involves the concepts of sustained effort, high failure rates, and uncertain outcomes.

Having a business plan in place gives you an outline of what to do and how to plan and achieve an idea in the future. Typically, these plans outline the first three to five years of your business strategy. A startup is so named because it represents the initial stage of the business. Initially, the funds come through the founder or cofounders and they tend to attract outside investors to grow.

Funding sources include family and friends, venture capitalists, crowdfunding, and loans. Startups must take into consideration their location and the legal structure. Though there is always a chance of failure, startups are presently booming owing to their unique plans of marketing, their innovative ideas, digitization, and the online mode of doing business. Creating a unique idea is the stepping stone of a startup.

Considering the Forbes India market analysis report, there have been 89 unicorns added in India till January 2022, and surprisingly, 41 of them had already entered the stable in 2021 alone. The speed with which startups are coming up in the Indian market is astonishing, to say the least. It would be quite interesting to learn the reason for this huge jump from a mere 29 unicorns between September 2011 and March 2020. Many ideas have been unique right from their inception; however, not every startup turns into a Unicorn.

Any startup that reaches the valuation of $1 billion is named a Unicorn. The term was first coined by Aileen Lee, founder of Cowboy Ventures. It was initially used to emphasize the rarity of such startups and although the definition of a unicorn startup has remained unchanged, the number has certainly increased. As per recent statistics, the pre-COVID era witnessed a total of three unicorns per year; however, 2021 has seen approximately four unicorns per month. This drastic rise has raised many questions for business and market analysts regarding the startup ecosystem of India. Are we Indians becoming more inclined to transform our passion to do business into a vision to solve an existing problem?

Even if the business idea seems feasible enough on market analysis, one of the most important hurdles for a startup revolves around funding. Savings, friends and family, or angel investors: there are umpteen choices available. Certainly, the financial backers would be more interested in putting their money into the unicorns; however, let me tell you, they often rely on smarter yardsticks such as the ability of companies to generate and compound free cash flow consistently as against the gross merchandise value.

In India, the startup list is growing with each passing day and the progress on the actual growth metrics is keenly watched. There is now a broader lens to scrutinize the valuation and value creation. Companies that could create efficient cash flow engines while ensuring top-quality governance have attracted investors and capital seamlessly.

Thus, if you harbor the desire to transform your startup dream into a unicorn someday, you must understand the 3C's of business—*Cash Flow, Communication, and Culture*. No matter how good your idea is, a regular cash flow is imperative to make the business run. A company's valuation takes the center stage only in the stock market, whereas a regular cash flow is essential to carry out day-to-day activities. You may get investors based on your unique idea; however, their patience will soon wane if your company fails to demonstrate the ability to create profits, growth, and cash flows. For example, private equity (PE) players are acquiring companies at unrealistic valuations; however, a reversal in the interest rate is likely to reverse their interest in such companies too. Any startup is watched for its sustainable growth along with the conduct of the company and its founders.

Whenever a startup has transformed into a public company, the market regulators and the public have kept a watchful eye. A startup must produce its vision concisely to enhance comprehension of the idea and in turn, evoke interest. A dearth of clarity is a warehouse of confusion and certainly impacts your business. The 3C's of business are interlinked to each other. To increase the cash flows, founders must develop clear communication and a great culture that is driven by values, ownership, accountability, and a sense of pride in the organization.

The present arena of business encourages hybrid work culture to bring in new ideas by incorporating the culture of cohesiveness, clarity, and inclusiveness. Every employee is empowered to represent the company and become a true ambassador for the startup's vision and mission. This new domain of startups involves a great blend of power and responsibility.

And if the founders learn the magic of the 3Cs, understanding and progressing in the startup business is not rocket science anymore. *"Given the amount of capital flowing into India, founders, today, are rushing to scale teams and their business. But the focus needs to be on the right processes or culture building for the long-term to avoid the pitfalls that may come in 2022 and beyond,"* said Nitin Sharma, the founding partner of Antler India, who was one of the most active venture capital investors during 2021.

Does the process stop after securing funds? No. Receiving funds for your startup is like getting the chance of procuring the raw resources. It has to be followed by registering your business and obtaining the required licenses or permits. Once the legality is formalized, you need to establish a business location. And then begins the marketing strategy, which involves creating an advertising plan to attract customers, establishing a customer base, and constantly adapting to the market demands. Starting a company is indeed a difficult venture but a rewarding one. Having a great idea and attempting to bring it to the market comes with a host of challenges, such as attracting capital, hiring employees, marketing, legal work, and managing finances. And yet, startups provide increased job satisfaction and the possibility of leaving a legacy.

What Is Scalability?

Any scalable business focuses on improving the profitability and efficiency of its services even if means an increase in the workload. Understand and improvise on the business's structure and strategize your workflow with a set of leaders with the necessary technical know-how. The scalability of a business more often depends on the effectiveness of communication, whether internally to the workforce or externally to clients and investors. Brand messaging should be consistent enough to help the public understand and like the product. If you wish to make your startup scalable, never reduce the scope of brand messaging. Why do you think Yahoo is lost in the game?

It lost its grip on the market after an abrupt growth that helped it expand while losing scalability. Scalable businesses must have sufficient tools for scaling evaluation. The tools facilitate the assessment and facilitation of scalability at every level. Thus, operational efficiency increases significantly. Capital budgeting comes in handy in a scalable business than it does in a non-scalable one. A scalable startup is one that begins with a lucrative and innovative idea and adopts a profitable business model that can grow quickly into a hugely profitable company. It has to enter a large market and create a niche for the company's products. It then poses significant competition to the incumbent businesses in the same industry and locality.

What Is Startup Ecosystem?

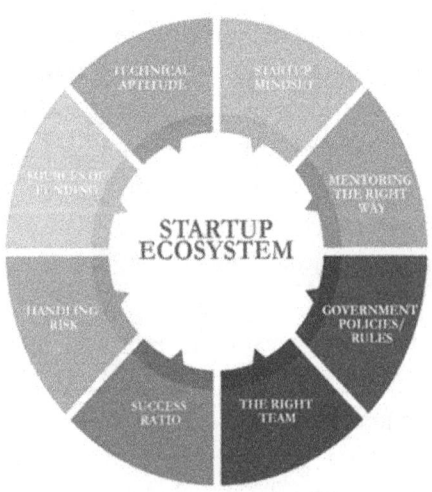

An ecosystem comprising of a group of people, startups, and related organizations that work to create and scale new startups is defined as Startup Ecosystem. Often formed in a relatively limited area, a startup ecosystem draws together key actors and stakeholders who incline toward growth ventures.

It includes new entrepreneurs, mentors, incubators, sources of talent such as universities and corporations, investors, and supporting services like startup-savvy law and accounting agencies. The startup ecosystem supports you with capital from investors and other entities, providing funding if your business idea sounds profitable for them. Along with the monetary help, such an ecosystem acts as a reservoir of knowledge and experience for an entrepreneur.

We are thriving in an era of unprecedented innovation and disruption through the undisruptive surge of startups, furnished with transformative products, business models, and capital to take on the world. Do you know that India is the third-largest startup ecosystem globally (numerical data) with more than 15,000 startups established in 2020? The major facilitators for this startup ecosystem are smartphone and internet penetration, cloud computing, application programming interfaces (APIs), and a national payments stack in place.

Additionally, the COVID-19 pandemic offered new avenues to encroach. India has seen a record rise in the number of unicorn startups. On the same note, it is NOT a cakewalk to be a unicorn. The unicorns of the present year have their own story with a list of features that worked in their favor. Some of the common features amongst all the unicorns are as follows:

- ➢ **Disruptive Innovation:** Mostly, all the unicorns have brought a disruption in the field they belong to. For example, Flipkart changed the concept of purchasing in India.
- ➢ **The Firsts:** Unicorns are more like starters in their industry considering the biggies as main course. They change the way people do things and gradually create a necessity for themselves. They are also seen to keep innovation up and running to stay ahead of competitors who might later boom. For example, Pharmeasy and Cure.fit.

- **Tech-savvy:** Another common trend across unicorns is that their business model runs on tech. For example, Vedantu, Meesho.
- **Consumer-focused:** 62% of the unicorns follow the B2C model of doing business. Their goal is to simplify the business transactions for the consumers and be a part of their daily affairs.
- **Affordability:** Startups attract their customers by offering alluring and affordable rates. For example, Spotify has made listening to music easier for the world.
- **Privately owned:** Most of the unicorns are privately owned whose valuation increases as a bigger business giant invests in them.

Do you know that 87% of unicorn products are related to software, 7% are related to hardware, and the rest 6% are other products and services?

Case Study: 1mg.com Startup Story

The idea of an online pharmacy or mail-order pharmacy is to provide healthcare facilities (medicines, doctor consultation, and diagnostic tests booking) over the Internet. 1mg is a digital consumer healthcare platform, or an online pharmacy center, that makes healthcare accessible, understandable, and affordable. 1mg.com was launched in April 2015 after Healthkart separated its generic drug search business, HealthkartPlus, and rebranded it as 1mg to allow users to find information about medicines prescribed by doctors and also buy it online.

Users can find medicines according to ailments, class of drugs, companies, and even particular brand names. There is a provision to upload your prescription and get the prescribed medicines. In case, the prescribed brand is unavailable, 1mg.com helps the patients with an alternative brand.

With artificial intelligence (AI) being hailed as the technology of the future, every startup is trying to adapt it in some capacity to streamline and optimize its offerings. 1mg.com recently started offering a feature, 'Ask a Doctor,' which is an intuitive chatbot that asks questions to accurately identify the user's health issue and suggests the medical specializations under which the ailment may fall. Users can choose from one of them and a doctor, who can diagnose the problem via chat, is assigned to the user.

1mg.com makes money with online diagnostics and lab testing services, and these contribute the maximum toward their annual revenues.

Online medicine delivery, B2B healthcare solutions, and subscription-based care plans make up the rest of their yearly finances. Apart from the main business plan of online pharmacy and diagnostic care, they also have native ads on their platforms for pharma companies to generate revenues. 1mg.com has expanded its pharmacies to 600 cities and also expanded its product range to include homeopathy and Ayurveda medicines. 1mg.com has raised a total of $204.6 million in funding over 16 rounds. Their latest funding was raised on April 19, 2021, from a Debt Financing round. 1mg.com is funded by 17 investors. International Finance Corporation and MAF Mauritius are two recent investors. The most recent investor has been TATA Digital as the investment in 1mg.com has been in line with the Tata group's vision of creating a digital ecosystem that addresses consumer needs across categories in a unified manner.

E-pharmacy, e-diagnostics, and teleconsultation are critical segments in this ecosystem and have been among the fastest-growing segments in this space, as this sector enabled access to healthcare through the pandemic. The overall market is around $1 billion and is expected to grow at ~50% CAGR driven by increased health awareness among consumers and greater convenience. This online healthcare tech is now an integral part of Tata Digital's ecosystem offering.

Date	Round	Amount	Lead Investors
April 19, 2021	Debt Financing	$13.3M	Tata Digital Group
Jan 31, 2020	Venture Round	$9.48M	Bill & Melinda Gates Foundation
Jun 28, 2019	Series D	$70M	Corisol Holding AG, International Finance Corporation
Apr 5, 2019	Series D	$10.3M	Redwood Global Healthcare Fund
Jan 1, 2019	Venture Round	-	InnoVen Capital
Mar 1, 2018	Series C	$10.1M	Maverick Ventures
Jul 26, 2017	Series C	$15M	HBM Healthcare Investments AG
Jun 30, 2017	Venture Round	$10M	HBM Healthcare Investments AG, Sequoia Capital India
May 31, 2016	Venture Round	-	HBM Healthcare Investments AG

How Do You Plan Your Startup?

Let me ask you in simple terms. Are you planning to make a Lifestyle Startup? Or are you planning to join the Self-employed clan, where you can live your preferred life while working for no one, but yourself? The idea is good, but not great enough to make a mark in the market until you become a top-notch performer in your domain.

You can obviously opt for the Small Business Startup while sticking to the traditional scope of doing business to feed your family. Well! Good enough to earn a living, but what if you can innovate a little and churn out a scalable business?

Let us have a short case study on Chai Sutta Bar founded by Anand Nayak and Anubhav Dubey. I would urge the younger generation not to grumble about hailing from a typical Indian middle-class family where your parents urge you to prepare for government jobs and competitive exams to make your life financially secure. Not everyone is destined to have a great score in CAT or UPSC. But life does not stop there and one of the brightest examples is Chai Sutta Bar founded by Anubhav Dubey and Anand Nayak. Although they failed to clear any of the prestigious examinations of our country, they walked on a different trajectory but with traditional thought.

Their business idea was common, old, and could be found on every street corner. They started their entrepreneurship journey with Chai, the most common beverage consumed by Indians after water. But they chose an unusual name to grab the eyeball. And these young entrepreneurs have come a long way while scaling more than 200 outlets in 100 cities in India. Five of the outlets are owned by the company and the other 195 are franchisee models.

They chalked out a different avatar through the price they offered and the way chai was served. Their target audience was the masses who could enjoy chai in their outlet for a mere Rs 10. They reintroduced the concept of kulhad and this brought financial support to 500 potter families. The cumulative sales from all their outlets stand at Rs 100 crore. January 2022 marks the second anniversary of their first overseas outlet in Dubai where their target customers are Indians, Bangladeshis, and Pakistanis. They offer a variety of flavors ranging from masala chai to kesar chai and chocolate chai. They could transform their traditional business idea with innovative cost management and marketing strategies.

So, let me ask again—Are you planning for a Scalable Startup: Born to Be Big?

The vision is to bring about a change. Such startups hire the best and the brightest and always search for a repeatable and scalable business model. When they find it, they start to look for more venture capital to boost their businesses. And then there is another option of Buyable Startups: Born to be bought.

Tech-based startups that offer web and mobile app solutions are often sold to larger companies. This tendency is becoming increasingly popular and their goal is not to build a billion-dollar company, but to be sold to a larger company in exchange of cash.

Large Company Startups either Innovate or die. Large companies have a finite life duration. Changes in customer preferences, new technologies, legislation issues, and new competitors create pressure, forcing large companies to create new innovative products for new customers in new markets. One of the finest examples is Oswaal Books by Prashant Jain. With the onset of COVID-19, the education sector in India underwent a massive shift. As offline activities came to a halt, schools and other educational institutions have had to jump into the new mode of going online.

Digitization played a vital role in making the education sector thrive. Oswaal Books, which started its business in 1984, has witnessed the evolution in the education sector. It has more than 35 lakh books in circulation, which include textbooks and reference materials for competitive examinations. Sensing the new way of learning, Oswaal Books launched its test-preparation platform for high-school classes with the name of Oswaal 360 in September 2021 on a trial basis. Since its launch, it has been able to garner more than one lakh users.

Oswaal Books plans to penetrate deeper into the scope of online learning by launching an app to offer preparation material for the National Recruitment Agency Common Eligibility Test. Their focus is on making the app available in various regional languages to overcome language barriers. Oswaal Books exploited the benefits of technology to withstand the changing market scenario and chose to innovate over dying out.

Roshni Sanah Jaiswal of Jagatjit Industries makes another interesting story of survival strategy. Roshini Sanah Jaiswal is a third-generation entrepreneur who is running one of India's oldest liquor companies, Jagatjit Industries. During the pandemic, she launched a preventive healthcare segment, which makes sanitizers that have a 24-hour efficacy. The same business in spirits, albeit with a slight modification in the alcohol ratio, and voila! A completely new product to withstand the rough waters.

The last option is to go for Social Startups with a Mission to bring about a Difference. These founders are passionate and driven to make an impact. However, unlike scalable startups, their mission is to make the world a better place, not for wealth creation but to promote a social cause or idea. However, let me tell you here, a unique idea often attracts investment and can make any business scalable.

Are You Choosing The Correct Sector?

India currently stands third in the global list of the number of companies that have attained unicorn status. In the current startup scenario, although India is well behind the US and China, it is certainly ahead of the UK and Germany. While fintech and e-commerce companies have led this phenomenon and remained at the forefront of establishing the unicorn ecosystem, other sectors such as Edtech, food delivery, and mobility have also made significant contributions. India's changing reforms and policies toward startups and various government initiatives have helped the Indian startups to scale up. The inflow of forex especially from leading tech companies such as Facebook, Google, and Microsoft into the Indian startup ecosystem signals the immense potential of the domestic market. Technology has played a key role in the making of pioneer business models. Most of the unicorns have leveraged technology in all possible ways, from refining internal organizational processes to enhancing the value proposition for their customers, incorporating AI while imparting better customer service.

India's Next Batch of Unicorns and Their Sectors
(2021 Review)

Sector	Unicorns
Fintech	bankbazaar, CAPITAL FLOAT, CredAvenue, DRIP/c, Fi, Fino, InCred, kissht, Jupiter, KhataBook, LENDINGKART, mswipe, one card, open, navi, PayMate, ZENWORK, zest, Paytm Money
E-Commerce	BIZONGO, boAt, purplle, CarTrade, DealShare, elasticrun, FURLENCO, Jumbotail, LIVSPACE, wakefit, pepperfry
Enterprise Tech	capillary, MyGate, uniphore, whatfix, Hubilo, moengage, FarEye
Consumer Services	bookmyshow, HomeLane, FreshHome, zepto
Logistics	netradyne, PORTER, Shiprocket
Media and Entertainment	GAMES24, inshorts, trell, WINZO, zupee, Nazara
Healthtech	HealthifyMe, MEDGENOME, mfine, practo
Edtech	BrightCHAMPS, Classplus, Teachmint
Transport Tech	rapido, Zoomcar
Real Estate Tech	stanza living, square yards
Deep Tech	GreyOrange
Travel Tech	EaseMyTrip

Moreover, the circumstances such as lockdowns and social distancing pushed several businesses to shift from using conventional methods to entirely digitally-driven operations, thereby creating better avenues for market forces.

By leveraging new-age technologies such as artificial intelligence, the Internet of things, data analytics, big data, and robotics, several startups bridged the gaps caused by the changed market scenario. By the end of 2021, the Indian startup ecosystem has come up more like a revolution with $208 billion worth of value-creation by 89 unicorns, in turn creating 2.6 million direct and indirect jobs.

Let us understand that any small product-based business needs distributors like supermarkets and retail outlets to take the products to the consumers. It is the most conservative mode of selling your product where you are bound to share a great deal of profit with the wholesalers and retailers. However, if a business wishes to carve a direct relationship with the consumers, then they have to opt for unorganized door-to-door selling. It is indeed outdated; nevertheless, Raj Shamani's success story would make anyone consider this direct-to-customer (D2C) selling model. Similarly, Tool Tech Toolings by Sunil Kirdak makes an interesting case study of the B2B model. This is an ISO 9001:2015 certified company and it is equipped with Industry 4.0 for manufacturing of CNC and VMC, forge components, electrical assembly for automobiles, and manufacturer of fixtures, gauges, special purpose machines, and robotic automation. Some of his clients are top brands in the automobile industry, including Bajaj Auto, Honda, Yamaha, TVS, Volkswagen, Skoda, Royal Enfield, and Siemens.

Business Models for Startups

A business model helps to depict the problems existing in the society to open an avenue for your startup and also chalks out how to draw profits while reducing competition. It also helps in identifying the right customers: whether to target another business sector or a regular customer.

B2B Model (Business to Business): The essence of this model lies in two or more businesses making a profit from each other. The prevailing assumption is that every business must be a provider only.

The B2B model defines a different segment altogether wherein the businesses play the role of customers as well. In the B2B type of business model, the exchange of goods and services takes place between two or more businesses. The final consumer comes into play at a later stage. A huge chunk of B2B transactions takes place in the exchange of raw materials, wherein one business sources raw materials from another business to manufacture a new product. One of the finest examples is iPhones. Apple makes iPhones under their trademark but sources various chipboards from Samsung. Although they are rivals in mobile technology, they exploit the B2B model for their profits. B2B models often work out with comparable negotiating power.

There is always a specific legal counsel to define the guidelines, profit margins, and negotiating terms. Alibaba is a wholesale B2B marketplace that offers millions of products in over 40 major categories to its customers, which includes consumer electronics, machinery, and apparel. IndiaMART, IndiaTrade, and the recently launched Amazon Business are some of the recently added competitors of Alibaba; nevertheless, it will take some time to dethrone Alibaba in the B2B platform. Currently, Alibaba seems to be the choice destination for cross-border trade and helps with both small and medium-scale businesses worldwide. B2B companies address the pain points of other businesses.

If you wish to have this model for your startup, look out for the market deficiencies and provide a solution for them: for example, selling CRM Software to organizations to keep track of their sales leads, manage their sales cycles, and determine a cold-calling schedule or selling office equipment to companies who wish to upgrade their existing furniture.

B2B model is complex and can be executed in three different modes.

- Supplier Centric Model
- Buyer Centric Model
- Intermediary Centric Model

Supplier Centric Model	Buyer Centric Model	Intermediary Centric Model
Supplier sets up a marketplace and intends to sell his customized solutions to various businesses. The solutions are priced according to the needs of the client/buyer. Example: CISCO, CM.com	It includes big corporates with huge purchasing capacity and high-volume purchases. The company here sets up a portal, mostly online, to accept quotations from different sellers. The sellers approach the company with their quotations and the company holds the power to accept or reject the business proposition. Example: Walmart	Intermediaries in the marketplace are the ones who provide a common platform for Buyers and Sellers to come together and interact either in the form of transactions or plain communication. They maintain a database of buyers and sellers and their main goal is to profit from these associations. Example: IndiaMart, LinkedIn

However, every model comes with its own pros and cons and so does the B2B model.

Advantages	Disadvantages
Better market predictability and stability	Market is limited
Better sales with less competition	Involves a lengthy process of decision making
Lower costs due to effective supply chain management and automation	Inverted structure as consumers has more power while determining customization, specifications.

B2C Model (Business to Consumer): The process of selling a product or a service from a business to consumers/end-users is classified as the B2C model. Most companies that sell directly to consumers can be referred to as B2C companies.

For example: Selling customized designer T-shirts to customers as per their specifications or providing online dating services. Any business transaction where the consumer directly receives goods or services, such as retail stores, restaurants, and doctor's offices, is considered as B2C. Most e-commerce businesses use online platforms to connect their products with the consumers. Flipkart and Snapdeal sell different brands on their platforms and cater to the public directly. B2C startups have their own benefits of adaptability and flexibility. They can access the consumers' socioeconomic status and demographics with an expansive marketing guarantee and can put their product on the market. However, there are several variables to consider for B2C startup entrepreneurs. B2C startups must analyze the costs involved to incorporate warehousing, planning and designing, inventory network activities, supply chain operations, and marketing. The Indian Startup ecosystem has a majority of tech startups concerned with e-commerce and consumer products and services that follow this B2C model. In our Indian scenario, easing public service delivery and driving efficiencies in waste management, water purification, and renewable energy are some of the emerging trends. As per the economic survey, private investment in B2C startups is much higher than investment in B2B startups.

B2C startup entrepreneurs enjoy complete authority over each component of their business structure, be it operational or customer service. This implies the sheer need for thorough research to know and distinguish the correct channel for reaching their target customers. And if you are willing to jump into this sector, you must distinguish your specialty to avoid rivalry as B2C is more often open to the global market. B2C specifically tackles a typical issue like delivering the essentials to your doorstep: for example, Bigbasket. But, how did the idea prosper? The presumption is that customers are rarely aware of the problems until they receive a solution.

However, B2C startups often fall prey to trends. An unavoidable trend or change can undoubtedly blow your clients away. B2C startups must be ready for innovating their products and it remains like gambling where there is no guarantee. With an apparently dashing yet unwanted change, you may chase your customers toward the competition with your own hands. For example, Snapchat's new design made a visible reduction in millions of customers.

We have to remember that B2C customers are less inclined to spend a large amount of cash on a product. Thus, your target is to acquire more customers. In the case of the most widely recognized B2C applications, you need a group of free clients to arrive at a small paying elite. In short, in the B2C model, your product and your marketing should go viral. Moreover, for costly products, the decision of the customer is often influenced by other factors. And, as the B2C model does not translate to potential extra profit, they attract relatively fewer investors.

Based on the type of audience and mode of targeting, the B2C model can be executed through three different modes.

E-Retailing	Brick & Click Retail	Virtual Malls
As most of the consumers have an online presence these days, reaching them online is the cheapest and fastest mode. Businesses have realized this and have started setting up websites and marketing campaigns to reach and sell products to netizens.	The typical brick and mortar shops realized the potential of the Internet and have started reaching out to a wider audience by setting up websites for their shops. Example: TATA Croma began Tatacliq as its online store.	The concept is providing a shopping mall experience over the Internet. A website hosts several merchants, giving them a space on the web to showcase their products while charging a nominal fee from sellers to display and sell products.

B2C models of startups have the following pros and cons:

Advantages	Disadvantages
Lowest cost involved	Interaction is impersonal and limited through apps or emails
B2C businesses are available 24/7	Competition is huge
Direct contact and communication with the customers	Customer inhibitions for online purchases considering the online frauds and thefts

> **C2C Model (Consumer to Consumer)**

The C2C business model involves consumers selling directly to consumers. Does it sound new to you? Are you not forgetting the classified section of the newspapers? The recent and the best example of a C2C model is OLX. Their tagline of 'Bech-de' became a household name and consumers could sell anything ranging from a sofa to videogames directly to any other consumer.

Advantages	Disadvantages
Transaction is mutual and effortless.	Dearth of quality control.
A customer can become both seller and buyer.	Lack in cooperation.

> **D2C Model/Brands (Direct to Customer)**

There are companies that build their offering around direct digital marketing channels as opposed to selling through an online marketplace, retailer, or auction site. This concept has eliminated the middlemen and has been a boon to the startups helping them save substantially on distribution costs.

In the D2C retail model, the products are marketed, shipped, and sold directly to the consumer. Physical outlets by D2C brands are purposely designed to enhance brand awareness and customer engagement, encouraging more online sales. Brands need to follow a traditional supply chain where their products need to pass through distributors and retailers before reaching the customers.

D2C models/brands rely heavily on some of the following marketing strategies:

- Relying on Loyal Customers: Collecting testimonials from loyal customers and sharing them in the ads, social media, landing page, product pages, and other relevant locations. Friendly reviews attract more customers.
- Relying on SEO tools and Keyword research: The marketing teams of D2C models incline more toward SEO (search engine optimization) using essential keywords in their ads.
- Do you have anything unique? In the present times, every product faces competition within a few months of its launch. Sometimes unique offerings or low-price models can beat the reputed brands. Unique marketing tactics often help in building long-term relationships with customers.
- Relying on referrals: How many times have you referred a not-so-famous brand to your friends? Customers often become the best marketers of a product or a brand unknowingly.

Leaving aside the manageable disadvantages, D2C is gaining more attention with continual disruption happening in the supply chain. Some of the famous D2C businesses are Mamaearth, Pepperfry, Licious, etc. Fashion, Fitness, Home & Kitchen and health & Wellness are some of the biggest categories in D2C space. Most of the D2C brands in India are bootstrapped. The core idea in D2C industry is to start a brand, grow it to a certain level and then seek venture capital to make it big.

Advantages	Disadvantages
Omnichannel experience with full control from manufacturing to marketing	Order fulfillment faces a lot of competition from big giants like Amazon
Brand reputation is in your hand	A highly talented marketing team is needed
Truly and thoroughly understanding the customers	Competing with retailers becomes troublesome

> ## On-Demand Business Model

You can call it a model for instant gratification. The biggest example of this is Airbnb, Ola, and Trivago. They provide all the information about tickets and hotel rooms instantly.

Pros: Ease of use and convenience and low costs involved as freelancers form the major portion of the workforce.

Cons: Freelancers can often screw up and then there is a lack of physical presence.

> ## Freemium Business Model

It is a clever strategy to draw customers through a free product. For example, Dream 11 provides players to not only compete against each other but also gain profit or money when they invest money into their app.

Pros: Customers can experience the product for free initially to understand and analyze the product.

Cons: Your marketing tactics should be extremely persuasive.

The Making Of Unicorns

From being a mythological horse-like creature with magical powers to becoming a desirable name for every entrepreneur, the term Unicorn has crossed many oceans. Innovative twists to the traditional scope of business have made their journey possible.

Let us have a quick look at some of the biggest unicorns of different startup sectors in India.

Flipkart: While the pandemic has overturned almost every aspect of our lives, customers have switched to online shopping, and as per the statistics, business has escalated tenfold now. COVID-19 succeeded in causing a bizarre number of consumers to tilt toward online shopping considering several factors like availability, convenience, and safety.

Founded in 2007 and listed under one of the largest e-commerce brands across India, Flipkart had initially begun as an online bookstore, but as the firm's fame escalated, it grew and expanded its activities. Comprising more than 150 million products in 80 categories, Flipkart adopts social media platforms like Twitter, YouTube, and Instagram for promoting its items. Being a B2C model firm, it offers its users the freedom to select their sellers and items from an extensive assortment of options.

Flipkart presently stands at a valuation of 24.9 billion USD in the year 2020. The primary investment of 5,600 USD had been infused by the founders themselves, which was later followed by investments from Accel India and Tiger Global, with the latter being the key investor of the company. More investors like eBay, Axis Bank, Manhattan Venture Partners, Naspers, and Softbank Vision Fund joined in, while the biggest turning point for the platform came when Flipkart was acquired by Walmart for $16 billion, with Walmart acquiring a 77% stake in the company.

Flipkart has carved a niche that shall be remembered and recited by young enthusiastic entrepreneurs for many upcoming years.

Razorpay: Founded by Harshil Mathur and Shashank Kumar, Razorpay is a Bangalore-based fintech startup that has recently secured $100 million in Series D funding led by GIC, Singapore's sovereign wealth fund, along with Sequoia and our existing investors Ribbit Capital, Tiger Global, Y-Combinator, and Matrix Partners and entered the unicorn club. Their vision was to help every business accept digital payments and over the years, they have made huge strides toward making it a reality.

Urban Company: Abhiraj Bhal, Raghav Chandra, and Varun Khaitan started Urban Company as an all-in-one platform that helps users hire premium service professionals, from masseurs and beauticians to sofa cleaners, carpenters, and technicians. Urban Company has built a network of 40,000+ trained service professionals and has served over 5 million customers across major metropolitan cities around the world. "The service providers are the most atomic form of business units in our society. If India needs to grow, if consumers need to benefit, they have to be empowered." – Raghav Chandra, cofounder of Urban Company

The business model is transformed into a full-stack, fulfilment model. Following the full-stack approach signifies an extensive investment in Urban Company's partners in the context of training, micro-financing, and approaching branded products and tools, and this has been a success mantra for Urban Company.

What's In Store For The Future?

Presently, India hosts the world's third-largest startup ecosystem, which is growing rapidly with digital adoption, domestic consumption, demographics, and the development of technology platforms as favorable tailwinds. Indians are quite the gluttons for technology, which in turn has made $35-$36 billion of investment in the tech sector during 2021 alone. The pandemic created a further conducive situation for startups. The policy and the technology startup ecosystem converged resulting in unparalleled value creation. India's capital markets regulator, SEBI, eased regulations that allowed public participation and helped sustain the Indian growth story. Startups such as Nykaa, PolicyBazaar, and Zomato were listed on the stock markets with historic retail investment and almost 42 Indian startups joined the list of unicorns. Technology is now thoroughly democratized!

Metaverse everything – The amalgamation of Web 3.0 and Metaverse cashed in on the possibility of physical reality and virtual reality merging.

Cryptocurrency and blockchain – Non-Fungible Tokens (NFTs) have been the most prominent development globally. Even though the possibility of using cryptocurrency in lieu of money is still remote, blockchain (BC) technology has come to the forefront. NFTs are investible. Many startups are building product, business, and service models around this development and BC technology is being used in banking, business, and other mainstream areas.

Vertical e-commerce (VEC) – VEC platforms are specialized tech platforms for product groups, where individuals can easily access items of their choice and browse for alternatives, all at competitive prices. VECs build on their product depth and extreme specialization to offer exciting services to their ever-growing loyal consumer bases. In 2022, we expect to see an increased buzz around VECs and exciting new vertical offerings.

Financialization of the Internet – As Internet products and services increasingly move into the mainstream, financial services are becoming more embedded in every app. From BNPL (Buy Now Pay Later) and micro-savings to the creator economy and payments for gaming, fintech will soon become a natural part of every Internet workflow. Consolidation in tech-enabled sectors – Consolidation is a natural phenomenon as large companies raise capital and take out competitors, and many smaller players fall by the wayside. We saw this phenomenon in several spaces like edtech and health tech in 2021. In fintech, too, with capital infusion, there is room for the rapid growth of companies, continued disruption of the sector, and growing market share for the winners. Stand-out players in every vertical will take every opportunity to consolidate services and provide new features to their consumer base.

How Biggies Are Allured To Startups?

As you see in the previous case study, the latest investment in 1mg.com was made by none other than the business giant of India, TATA SONS. This 153-year-old conglomerate of India produces salt to steel and is the heritage of the Indian business world.

The startup ecosystem flourishes while established business houses invest in progressive ideas. Business is always a two-way path; to earn something, you must give as well. In this era of digitization and every minuscule aspect of business going online, staying relevant involves having the foresight to expand into newly-thriving industries and making shrewd acquisitions.

Although Tata is more inclined to traditional businesses, it had to cope in the fast-growing era of startups. It identified the growth-oriented innovations in the scope of online delivery of essentials and designed its startup acquisition spree.

- **BigBasket:** Tata Digital acquired a 64% stake. The company clocked gross sales of $1.1 billion or INR 8,000 crore in FY 2021.
- **CureFit:** Tata Digital invested $75 million and Mukesh Bansal, CEO of Cultfit & the founder of Myntra, joined Tata Digital.
- **1mg:** Tata Digital acquired a majority stake in the largest digital health platform in India.

A startup's profit-making score attracts investments and also helps with acquisitions. While established business houses always look for new ideas to diversify, startups can join the bandwagon to fund their ideas. Clearly, Tata has realized it is late to the startup party. To make amends, it is buying already scaled startups. More recently, Tata has launched a whole new app **Tata Neu** to encompass all the three acquisitions under the same app. That is, the customers need not have separate app for 1mg and BigBasket as they both will be made available within Neu app.

"The success of the young entrepreneur will be the key to India's transformation in the new millennium."
— Dhirubhai Ambani

Key Takeaways

- Scalability is essential for startups
- Learning the know-how of startup ecosystem
- Different business models possible for startups
- Future prospects of startup in India

As the essentialities of starting a startup are understood, let us scrutinize the significance of finding a suitable cofounder for your startup.

5

THE COFOUNDER CONUNDRUM

The dawn of a startup definitely begins with a great idea; however, no matter how great an idea is, efficient execution remains the key to its success. And the execution of any great plan needs a great team. An efficient team, inclined toward the startup mission, makes a world of difference to the startup. The startup ecosystem runs on the inevitable principle of having a cofounder alongside to build and run the business. But what about Vijay Shekhar Sharma of Paytm? How does one realize if there is actually a need for a cofounder? And before you jump the gun and hunt for a cofounder, consider the following factors. A cofounder must: burn equal skin in the business, be passionate about the idea as you are, bring diversity in skill and idea, not run away in times of adversities

> *"A good idea is worthless without impeccable execution and a commitment to iterate."* – Zach Klein

Your personality type and experience pave your need for a cofounder. If you are a collaborator who welcomes different opinions, then you are good to go for a cofounder. But, if you are individualistic, it is better to go solo. Similarly, there are a couple of benefits of having a cofounder that one cannot deny.

Cofounders often remain the storehouse of moral and emotional support. Startups require far more time and effort than a 9-to-5 job. With so much money on the line and changing scenarios of threats and opportunities, cofounders often impart emotional strength to swim through the rough patches.

Investors are more inclined toward companies that have diversified skills at the top. Why? Because it widens the scope of success. Decision-making skills are improved. Nobody likes a company that is run like a dictatorship. Decisions should be taken considering multiple dimensions and different perspectives. Cofounders come from different backgrounds and impart their unique outlook to the decision-making process. Remember, a difference of opinion always opens new avenues to look into. Bring in a cofounder to broaden your perspective.

Responsibilities can be divided. Running a company is not a cakewalk, especially when the company is in the initial phases. A cofounder helps to divide the stress and responsibility associated with running a startup. The presence of a cofounder contributes toward a better work-life balance. Much like in a traditional business, startups, too, need complementary skills amongst the cofounders. Different backgrounds translate to different viewpoints and each cofounder can handle a department suited to his/her skillset.

Risk is often mitigated as both profit and loss are shared. Having multiple founders means greater stability in the minds of the investors. After obtaining a degree in your hands and a few years of experience in the field, you may end up thinking of yourself as a master of all trades. However, you are bound to get a reality check soon. It is vital for you to associate with like-minded people who can complement your skills and take your business to heights that would not have been possible with only you handling all the affairs.

On the same note, cofounders should have detailed discussions, structured and otherwise, to understand their different styles of working and they MUST NOT avoid discussing the finances and equity.

Which Cofounder Shall Become The CEO?

When two cofounders come together, the one who has better communication skills and greater access to venture capitalists becomes the CEO.
You can become the CEO of your startup if you have the following qualities/abilities:

- A good storyteller with the ability to make people believe in your idea.
- A problem solver, both at an organizational and emotional level.
- Strategy foreseer. You should be able to see the impact of today's decision over the years to come.
- Able to inspire and motivate others toward the company's mission.
- A team worker.
- Capacity to empathize and be a true leader.

In the world of startups, staying relevant is the key to success. In fast-growing startups, the roles and the skills needed keep changing rapidly. It is the duty of the CEO and the other cofounders to ensure they have a development plan and the support to help all cofounders scale up their skills and capabilities to fit the growing demands of a high-growth startup. As the gears change from early-stage to growth, cofounders must assess the need for diversified skills. The main job of a startup cofounder is to keep the training and development plans active forever. Preventive steps are always better than corrective measures.

The Ideal Number Of Cofounders

This concept of finding out the ideal number of cofounders has been a center of study for experienced business economists. However, there has been no conclusive end. Some studies indicate that startups with two cofounders have fared better than the others who had four or more cofounders. While many studies put the chosen business model as the criteria to select the number of cofounders needed. Considering the outlook of venture capitalists, it is optimum to have at least two cofounders. Having multiple cofounders adds credibility to your business and it has been recommended that there should be three cofounders. This helps with the tie-breaking vote while moving ahead with a decision. Choose your cofounders by considering their investment value, core values, and reliability. Sometimes, it is not more the merrier. A greater number of cofounders raise more issues pertaining to equity. All cofounders should also decide on an entrusting schedule and related terms before incorporation and registration. The terms should be fair and must prevent future dissatisfaction in the company.

The Founding Dilemma

"If you give a good idea to a mediocre group, they'll screw it up. If you give a mediocre idea to a good group, they'll fix it. Or they'll throw it away and come up with something else."
Ed Catmull

There is a famous saying in the world of business that a rising tide lifts all the boats. As India declares January 16 as the National Startup Day, the younger generation must realize the need for plunging into the role of job creation. Every startup must conceive the idea of a strong founding team that can strive with vision and ambition to explore the product/market fit and carve a niche for themselves amongst the competition.

The size of the market and the defensibility of the product turn into the main drivers during the stage of scaling up. It is the time to morph visionary planning into strategic execution. Every startup goes through the founding dilemma; however, if you consider any successful startup, their diversified and skilled founding team would have played a crucial role across the company's lifecycle.

It is a huge commitment to choose an ideal founding team and every entrepreneur must rush to it. As stated earlier, the founding team is a crucial element in a startup's success and any changes to the structure of the founding team can lead to the biggest crisis for a startup. The focus drifts away from the market and the product during such a dilemma. Do you know that identifying and addressing gaps in the core team is always easier than replacing a founder?

You have to remember that your founding team should be designed based on the product you create. Cofounders who are good at marketing can come on board at a later stage if your startup is focused on developing payment apps. One of the cofounders must be a specialist in the field of app designing. The founding dilemma is often eliminated once you broaden the horizon of your search.

The founding team must maintain the team dynamics by keeping to the following principles.

- Disagreeing on the short-term objectives throws up a red flag. A long-term vision is difficult to achieve at the inception stage and thus, every cofounder must have a 12 to 18 months execution plan ready.
- Actively nurture the culture of discussing even the most peculiar ideas.
- Accepting the changing scenario is an asset for the founding team. The team needs to be able to move from one go-to-market obstacle to another and find a good balance between smart iteration and panicked pivoting.
- Sticking to high recruiting standards is the most difficult part of scaling a business. Smart recruiting and related headhunting require a lot of effort and are the key

denominators in successful early-stage companies. High recruiting standards often go hand in hand with an ambitious vision and high-performing operations.
- ➢ Keeping the focus on the expansion of activities.
- ➢ Planning and strategizing must lead to systematic execution across sales and operations. Ideas need execution; otherwise, they are just equal to a vanishing dream.

There are cases where team dynamics have changed in due course of time. Some innovative founders might only be interested in founding companies, and not in the scaling-up process. This is not a good sign in the overall entrepreneurship journey. Why? Because a visionary leader is needed during the inception; however, becomes a disaster during the scaling stage. Thus, the founding team must undergo restructuring of responsibilities in different phases of the business. No founding team carries all the capabilities to run a business. Every cofounder must be aware of the loopholes left and should strategically work to fill in the gaps with suitable talent.

Scrutinize yourself first before you start headhunting for a suitable cofounder. Are you aware of your skills and superpowers? Moreover, have you identified your weaknesses? Once you are able to identify your strengths and weak points, you have to search for someone who complements you. Your ideal cofounder must possess the skills you lack. Possess the right mindset while looking for a cofounder. Your aim is to make your business idea work. Finding the perfect cofounder is all about good fortune: widen your area of search to increase your chances of finding the perfect cofounder. Time spent discussing and threshing out your ideas also aids in identifying the perfect cofounder. You must remember before giving the heads-up for a potential cofounder that there is a strong and honest foundation in your relationship; this is very crucial.

There is a popular culture of 3H while cofounding a startup. A startup should have a Hipster, a Hacker, and a Hustler amongst its cofounders. The Hipster designs the product or service, the Hacker builds it, and the Hustler sells it.

The 3H concept is structured on the belief that complementary skill sets are critical amongst the cofounders to effectively build and scale a company. Does that mean you need 3 cofounders? For example, one cofounder can be the Hustler and the Hipster, and the other could be the master building the product. Similarly, while choosing the cofounder, analyze if the chosen cofounder is going to be an energy-gainer or energy-drainer. The startup journey is not a bed of roses and it is important for you and your cofounder to do fact-analysis often. On the same note, the cofounder must be a motivator and problem solver and not the other way around.

Building a Startup from Scratch

Assembling a proper team for a new and emerging startup is a critical aspect of beginning your business career. A startup forms and goes through different stages.

Garage Era: While startups are built on the concept of innovation, millennial entrepreneurs often name the inception stage the Garage Era. The founding team often has an executive officer, a technology officer, and a sales and marketing officer. The CEO is often considered as the dreamer in any startup because he/she conceives the ideologies needed. The CTO remains the engineer who designs and incorporates the changing trends of technology around. The sales and marketing cofounder acts as the hustler who taps on the growth hacks. While the 'sales' side has to focus on revenue generation, the marketing aspect covers the prospective customers.

Scale-Up Era: Now, if every aspect is taken care of by the founding team, when does a startup create jobs? The answer— during the Scale-Up Era. The hiring process begins here when a multiskilled workforce is needed to stay adaptable in the face of rapid change. People with diverse skills are hired and put to multiple activities. At this stage, a financial officer, a business development manager, and a customer service representative are hired.

Opening the Big League: At this stage, the startup must incorporate a product team, a design team, and an engineering team. A Product Manager is one of the most crucial hirings you can make as a startup founder if you wish to grow quickly. As you progress through your first year, you will start with a concept, validate it, transform it into a great product, and then scale it into a lucrative business.

Your Product Manager must be familiar with all elements of the product and must be aware of the issue you are trying to solve. He/she has to put your suggested solution to the test against a carefully constructed hypothesis, and iterate small, measured modifications to your product. And in this role, the Product Manager must have a thorough awareness of all the facets of the problem and guide the product from the concept stage to a fully-fleshed-out solution that answers your customer's needs.

The design team brainstorms and implements ideas on product functionality and studies how the user interacts with the product, the look of the product, and the product behavior within frames. Different specialties such as UX, animation, illustration, and more are needed in this team. This collaborative team spearheads the smooth running of the project. The engineering team is flexible and cross-functional and its members pool their skills and knowledge to create components that are reliable, reusable, and testable. Strengthening internal relationships amongst your team members as well as external ties with other organizations and customers is a primary priority for any startup.

Your organization will lack direction and effective leadership if these positions are not filled. In reality, management problems account for 65 percent of all firm failures. That is why it is critical to begin at the ground-up and then grow your staff as your resources allow. It is imperative to think about your company's aims and beliefs when filling these positions.

Hiring the right people is tricky. As a cofounder, you must seek people who can help you enhance your leadership and appropriately represent your brand.

Organizational Structure Of A Startup

At the inception stage, when the team is small, a lack of role clarity is permitted as it can increase the team's agility. Problems are sorted out by the person who finds them. It is indeed cumbersome but still acceptable during the initial days. However, as the company grows, there comes the need for a proper organizational structure. Specialists are inducted to professionalize each area of the business, and the hierarchy is drawn to ensure information flows up and down the organization, enabling the CEO to remain accountable.

The current era of business is unafraid of including technology. With digitization becoming an integral part of doing business, it is easier to dissect the organizational structure of a tech-startup to understand the distinct roles of the team members.

CEO: The role of the CEO is to set the vision, build a great leadership team, and give them the resources they need to succeed. No founder starts as a 'pure' CEO, but as an operator. Gradually they start delegating to make room for strategic thinking, recruiting, team coaching, and managing key relationships with investors and partners. When there are just two cofounders, the term co-CEO can be used, but it is never a good idea. The concept of co-CEO eventually leads to power struggles, stalemates, and conflicts. There are cases when investors opt to have a single CEO as a requirement for investing.

COO: Operations get the business model and the operating system to work together. The COO is often the CEO's right hand, filling in where the CEO cannot. They usually lead all non-product operations and project management, and they also carry out functions pertaining to HR, finance, and legal aspects during the initial stages of the startup.

Head of Product: The objective is to understand the customer needs and translate them into valuable, usable, and feasible product requirements. The Head of Product leads a team that includes customer researchers, rapid prototypers, designers, data analysts, and product owners.

Technology Head: He/she heads a team that is focused on developing a reliable, scalable, and high-quality tech-based product. You might find front-end engineers, back-end engineers, data scientists, system architects, and dev-ops on this team.

Growth Team: Growth teams usually take an experiment-based approach to understand the growth rate of the product. The team is often composed of product managers and engineers, as well as performance marketers and SEO experts.

Marketing Team: The business-to-customer marketer focuses on building awareness and desire for the product or service. The team includes personnel from customer research, paid marketing, customer relationship management (CRM), and brand marketing. While the B2B marketing team takes care of the event marketing and design for the strategic partnerships.

Sales Team: Sales is often split into two parts: sales development and account execution. This team is directly responsible for selling the company's product or service to the ideal customer profile.

CFO: Managing the finances is a huge task. The CFO looks after the financial strategy, which includes the business model and pricing through to the optimal funding balance between operating cash flow, debt, and equity. They oversee accounting, treasury, compliance, statutory and investor reporting, financial modeling, and fundraising operations. Startups, at the early stage, do not need a CFO as the CEO looks after fundraising and investor relations. The accounting is generally outsourced. A more strategic CFO is needed in later stages when your financing becomes more complex and you start making acquisitions or you widen the internal finance function.

HR Manager: The focus is to hire, fire, and manage employee performance. A startup proliferates and grows with the right organizational structure that aligns with the business strategy. The founders or the CEO need to carefully decide where to place the resources to fashion the competitive edge. Each layer in the hierarchy is chosen to manage and execute their plans independently.

Significance of Technical Cofounders

Human life is now ruled by technology. Whether you wish to buy a kitchen appliance through Flipkart or book a movie ticket online, you are surrounded by technology.

India has witnessed a drastic change while making technology a part of our daily lives. Almost every business, whether a traditional grocery shop or a startup, has a dangling unit of digital payment or a mobile app. Even if you only want to start a simple restaurant or a cozy bed and breakfast in a small hill station, you will still need to build an application to make your business operations smoother. Post- demonetization and COVID-pandemic, it has become imperative to install technology in any business to keep it running through the changing market scenario.

As chalked out previously, differently skilled cofounders are always an asset to a startup. For example, a technical cofounder can handle the founder-level responsibilities such as setting a long-term mission and vision for your startup and strategizing ways to scale up and can also handle the technical sides of your business. A technical cofounder forms the premise of analytical thinking, which is truly essential to build the startup empire. Along with the splash of innovation and creativity, the technical cofounder introduces practicality toward scaling up the business.

Let us have a quick look at the benefits of having a technical cofounder.

- **Merging innovation with technology:** The intricate meshwork of your creativity must be sustainable in the digital world. A startup is often overwhelmed with new ideas, wild tangents of innovative strategies, and new campaigns. If creative thinking is the Yang for your startup, the technical cofounder takes the charge from the ideation phase to the development phase much more quickly and efficiently. They not only help you overcome seemingly complex obstacles with effective and easy-to-implement solutions, but will also play a huge part in the iteration process of developing your product or service. Thus, the technical cofounder helps in producing a balanced offering that will appeal to a wider range of audiences.
- **Business In and Out:** The technical cofounder strategizes the product and thus knows the business in and out. The technical cofounder can be your go-to for pitch presentations to impress and persuade investors to decide on future action plans to grow your business in different verticals. They often chalk out mergers and potential partnerships with other businesses.
- **Going Online:** Technology research, wireframe building, data migration, hosting server configurations, architecture development, implementation planning, and resource allocation become easy if the startup has a technical cofounder.
- Business operates smoothly in the presence of a technical cofounder.
- Technology is like the proverbial Hydra and it is evolving with each passing second. A technical cofounder can make your startup evolve with time.
- Presence of a technical cofounder increases the investors' faith in your startup.

It is vital to have a technical cofounder for a startup not only to help in simplifying the operational and financial aspects of building your startup, but also to bring in a valuable asset while scaling up the business. A technical cofounder is vested in the improvement of the technological side of the company. They share the same vision for the product and contribute whatever they can in the form of technical advice and improvements in the product. Remember, Steve Jobs was the entrepreneur while Wozniak was the technical wizard for Apple.

Diversity Rocks

"Business-heavy founding teams are 6.2x more likely to successfully scale with sales driven startups than with product-centric startups. Technical-heavy founding teams are 3.3x more likely to successfully scale with product-centric startups without network effects than with product-centric startups with network effects. Balanced teams with one technical founder and one business founder raise 30% more money, have 2.9x more user growth, and are 19% less likely to scale prematurely than technical or business-heavy founding teams."
-Startup Genome Report

If your startup team is comprised of members with the same skillsets as yours, then be confident that you have just multiplied your weaknesses.

Diversity breeds success; so, do not make the mistake of creating a team of similar skills. Cofounders are needed from all avenues to run the business successfully.

Case study: BigBasket – The Virtual Mall of Grocery Shopping

Bigbasket was launched with five founding members, not young but with enough experience and skills behind them. Hari Menon is the current CEO, and one of the founders of Bigbasket, who had also served as the CEO of IndiaSkills. He was the cofounder of Fabmall and had worked as the Country Head at PlanetAsia and Business Head at Wipro. The four other founding members of Bigbasket are Mr. VS Sudhakar, Mr. Vipul Parekh, Mr. Abhinay Choudhari, and Mr. VS Ramesh. They form an exclusive example of diversification of skills amidst the cofounders. Each of the founders has a unique vision about the business, and their ideas complement each other. Mr. Sudhakar has got a vast experience in the IT sector. Mr. Parekh is the Head of Finance and Marketing at Bigbasket, whereas Choudhari serves as the Head of New Initiatives. With 21 years of experience in the logistics sector of the Indian Navy, Ramesh is currently the Head of Logistics and Supply Chain of the company.

Their first online business was conceived as Fabmart.com in 1999. The online grocery division of this business was launched in 2001, and the company grew exceptionally. They also started a succession of grocery supermarkets called Fabmall in south India, which was later acquired by the Aditya Birla group in 2006 and rebranded as More. The founders had a staunch vision to establish something huge in the grocery market sector in India and finally launched Bigbasket in 2011. The company raised around $10 million in the first round of funding from Ascent Capital and by 2014, the company grew massively in three major cities, confirming over 5,000 orders every day. In March 2016, the company raised $150 million from Abraaj Capital in Series D funding and soon crossed 10 million customer orders and also received 1 million orders in a single month.

By June 2017, the company could raise around $290 million in total from 8 rounds of funding and 11 investors. The year 2017 saw Paytm and Alibaba become Bigbasket's main investors. With all the investments it received, Bigbasket decided to expand the business in the other cities of India, too. The company also built several warehouses and invested in cold room facilities to enhance its range of fresh products. It also invested in technology to make delivery more efficient and shopping easier, both from the browser and mobile applications. But amid the growing competition, Bigbasket focused on personalized shopping.

After five years of comprehensive research, Bigbasket figured out that the products in demand varied from city to city. This helped in including more brands, which escalated the profit of the company and helped outdo its rivals. Bigbasket aims to give the product at a lower price with a higher margin, as 35 percent of revenue comes from private labels. The company wants to fill the gap in the margin with other products such as organic food and high-end consumer products, to name a few. Moreover, the company also provides staples, fruits, and vegetables at a lower price. They also started a B2B side; they started serving Kirana Stores, huge corporates, and the HoReCa (hotels, restaurants, and cafés) sector. They aimed to extend their reach and cover the market by providing all the facilities, ensuring that customers would not have to go anywhere else for their needs except to Bigbasket.

Before Flipkart could become a household name, Fabmall was already hitting the wall of making purchases online. Today, Menon may not be the richest entrepreneur; however, Bigbasket proves that fortune does favor the brave, maybe not instantly but eventually.

The Risks Involved

A study at the University of Southern California, Marshall School, suggested that 65 percent of startups failed due to cofounder conflict. While 10 percent of cofounders break up in the first year of the startup, 45 percent fall apart after four years or more.

It is true that building a company is lonely and one needs emotional support. Moreover, there is a dire need for technical skills in the present times. Still, the constant emphasis on venture capitalists being withdrawn from solo founder startups is outdated. There are a couple of under-appreciated risks in going on a fanatic hunt for a cofounder.

Sometimes, in your urge to impress your investor with a cofounder, you end up choosing someone who is less dedicated than you are. So, you may end up wasting your time and energy. Have you heard of a shotgun wedding? Never opt for shotgun cofounding. Until you are sure that your compatibilities are aligned, do not enter into any business partnership. Competing vision is terrible for the business to progress. Divergent thinking is great, but only when communication allows for healthy conflict. Turning initial chemistry into a compatible partnership takes time. Do not be in a hurry.

Key Takeaways

- The importance of cofounding a startup.
- Organizational structure of a startup.
- Importance of diversely skilled cofounders.

"The challenge we face is in talent – it takes bandwidth and time to get talent and build a team."
–Bhavish Agarwal

Cofounders not only bring different perspectives to the table of growth but also lure investors. Let us have a look at the different modes to fund your startups in the next chapter.

6

THE FUNDING OF STARTUPS

Is the lack of money stopping you from pursuing your entrepreneurship dream? Worry not! The whole world seems to be humming the startup tune, and taking the plunge into a career that involves running a profitable business while simultaneously creating jobs has gained hallmark prominence across nations. With each passing year the number of startups is rising in developed economies, and in the present times, securing funds for your startup is never a problem.

> *"Startup India is an initiative to facilitate budding entrepreneurs. If the ecosystem sustains and multiplies then we are in the right direction."*
> – Nirmala Sitharaman

Your business idea can be innovative as well as provocative; however, one of the most essential elements for startup success is your ability to obtain sufficient funding to start and grow the business. There are many founders who have financed their new companies with their own capital or by borrowing money from family or friends. How can one forget the journey of the Emami Group?

The inception of the Emami Group took place during the mid-70s in West Bengal when two childhood friends, Mr. RS Agarwal and Mr. RS Goenka left their high-profile jobs as Chartered Accountants with the Birla Group to set up Kemco Chemicals, an Ayurvedic medicine and cosmetic manufacturing unit in Kolkata. The year was 1974 and the business began with a meager capital of Rs 20,000. It was an extremely bold step for a home-grown business entity during those days when the Indian FMCG market was still dominated by multinationals. They chose the time when the burgeoning Indian middle class had gained an increasing potential for consumption, and that assured a bullish trend in the personal care market in the mid-70s. Both Agarwal and Goenka, powered by their keen sense of consumer insight and business vision, realized the importance of the herbal revolution of Ayurveda and started manufacturing cosmetic products as well as Ayurvedic medicines under the brand name of Emami in 1974.

The term funding refers to the money required to start and run a business. A financial investment is essential toward product development, manufacturing, expansion, sales and marketing, office spaces, and inventory. To escape from the risk of debts and equity dilution, there are many startups that choose to not raise funding from third parties and are funded by their founders only. However, additional investment becomes unavoidable when the startups plan to grow and scale-up. Startup funding is crucial but never easy and takes a longer time than anticipated.

Why Startups Need Funding?

A startup is about setting the first foot into the world of business. There is a multitude of aspects where a startup needs funding; however, every entrepreneur must be clear with a detailed financial and business plan before they approach anyone for funds. A startup may require funding for the following purposes:
- Prototype creation
- Product development

- Working capital
- Procuring raw materials and human resources
- Office space and admin consultation
- Legal certification, licenses, etc.
- Marketing and sales

Getting your startup off the ground is the first step and before you approach any funding agency to fund your business idea, you must have a detailed business plan. A budding entrepreneur must have a clear understanding of the business operation. Any investor would like to see your financial projections before investing in your idea.

A thorough description of your business and operative methods, the distinct role of each cofounder and your team, and financial prognoses are some of the major points that the funding agencies/investors would look for. You must have your financial projections ready for three to five years down the line. Always remember that you cannot make a profit from day one; however, you can be accurate while predicting your finances.

Why Would Anyone Invest in Startups?

At the brink of your entrepreneurship, this is a common doubt that might haunt you. Why would any outsider be interested to fund your idea? Before I engage you with the various modes of securing funds, let me clear this doubt. Any financial investment works out with an intention to earn profit. Investors essentially buy a piece of the startup company as they proceed with the investment. They put down their capital, in exchange for equity, i.e., a portion of ownership in the startup and rights to its potential future profits. Investors come into a partnership with the startups in which they invest. When the startup turns a profit, investors make returns proportionate to their amount of equity in the startup. On the same note, if the startup fails, the investors lose the money they have invested.

Investors can realize their return on investment from startups through various means of exit. Usually, the venture capitalist firm and the entrepreneur discuss the various exit options at the beginning of investment negotiations. A well-performing, high-growth startup that works with an excellent management system and carries a well-planned organizational process is more likely to be exit-ready than other startups would be. Venture Capital and Private Equity funds usually exit all their investments before the end of the fund's life.

Investors look for nine critical features in a startup before they consider investing.

- ➢ **Startup objective:** Any investor would see the problem-solving ideation and capacity of a startup. Is your startup capable of meeting specific customer needs? Moreover, ideas or products that are patented show high growth potential for investors.
- ➢ **Scope of scalability and sustainability:** Startups with the potential to scale and remain sustainable in the near future attract investors. They carry a stable business plan with accurate financial prognoses and thus investors can rely on them easily. While chalking out scalability and sustainability, they often consider barriers to entry, initiation costs, growth rate, and expansion plans.
- ➢ **Team:** The personal attributes of the management team contribute a lot toward attracting investors. The passion, experience, and skills of the cofounders and the efficacy of the management team to drive the company forward are crucial to invite investment.
- ➢ **Market setting:** Investors often look for the kind of market the startup is targeting. Having a myopic outlook with respect to the market size or focusing on an exclusively localized market would not be a good idea. Investors watch for obtainable market share, product adoption rate, historical and forecasted market growth rates, and

macroeconomic drivers in a startup's target market.
- **Customers and suppliers:** Your vendors and customers shall be scrutinized by the investors.
- **Scope of competition:** Investors do check the vulnerability of your product against the competing market. The startup must create the true picture of the competition and the other players in the market working on similar things for the investors. There can never be an apple-to-apple comparison but highlighting the service or product offerings of similar players in the industry is important.
- **Financial projections:** A detailed financial business model that showcases cash inflows over the years, investments required for the key milestones, break-even points, and growth rates must be produced to the investors. The startup must communicate a realistic assumption.
- **Marketing strategy:** No matter how good your product or service may be, if it does not find any end-use, it is no good. Before you approach a potential investor, ensure that you have chalked out the sales forecast, targeted audiences, product mix, conversion and retention ratio, etc. A foolproof sales and marketing strategy infuses confidence in the investors.
- **Exit options:** The showcasing of potential future acquirers or alliance partners by the startup turns out to be a valuable decision parameter for the investors. Initial public offerings and acquisitions and subsequent rounds of funding must showcase the exit options.

Here, I would emphasize that no investor ever burns money mindlessly. Investors make smart investments to gather a win-win situation.

"As a startup, one must go after money which understands the business."
– Sachin Bansal

Considering the emerging economies of the world, India is the new face for startup investment. The last decade has witnessed some major startups disrupting the conventional corporate scene in India. A startup is more like a million-dollar baby; however, every startup crafts a different story of success or failure. The competition is huge, but so are the growing opportunities to diversify. In India, almost every fortnight when a new startup gears up to begin operations, another one falls apart. Funding has been one of the colossal steps to ponder for every startup. Launching a startup definitely goes a long way in healing the wound of unemployment for a densely populated country like India. Similarly, it is indeed an absolute advantage if your creation is innovative and self-motivated; nevertheless, the idea must be satisfactorily funded at the different stages of the business growth. Startup funding becomes a herculean task, especially at the ideation and development stage when the venture would need funding for more than a couple of rounds. Unless a startup consistently makes profits for a good six to seven months, it is difficult to handle the payoffs, operations, and other utilities without a constant cash flow. Investment helps in operating the startup smoothly and successfully.

Types Of Startup Funding

One of the most common terms in the funding avenues is **Working Capital.** The simplest way to define working capital is 'the funds required to meet day-to-day expenses like wages, rent, and electricity and water charges, and for investment in the current assets, such as stock of raw materials, semi-finished goods, and finished goods. Working capital is often known as the circulating capital because the investments in the current assets are recovered and reinvested repeatedly in due course of business operations. Working capital can be gathered through short-term funds. However, running a business is a continuous process and the startup must have a certain amount of working capital at all times.

The sheer need for working capital as well as the amount is determined by the following factors:

- More working capital is needed if the cost of raw materials covers the major portion of the total cost.
- Labor-intensive methods of production need more working capital.
- Higher investments must be procured for lengthier operational processes.
- If raw materials and other services are available on credit and goods produced are sold for cash, less working capital investment will be involved. On the other hand, if the raw material is to be purchased in cash and goods produced are sold on credit, larger working capital will be necessary.
- The faster the use of raw materials in the production process, the faster is the sale of goods produced, and the lesser the amount of working capital needed.
- Startups engaged in manufacturing seasonal goods are required to have a relatively larger amount of working capital to meet off-season requirements.

Now, the working capital can be obtained through the following methods:

1. Equity Financing: The process of raising capital through the sale of shares is known as equity financing. Companies raise money because they might have a short-term need to pay bills or have a long-term goal and require funds to invest in their growth. By selling shares, a company is effectively selling ownership in their company in return for cash. There is no concept of repayment of the invested funds. Moreover, there is no guarantee against the financier's investment, although the startup has to share a portion of its ownership. Equity Investors usually prefer to involve themselves in the decision-making process and there is indeed capital growth for the investors.

Sources of equity funding: Angel Investors, Self-financing from Family and Friends, Venture Capitalists, Crowd Funding Incubators/Accelerators, and also IPO (Initial Public Offering). An IPO is a process through which a private company can offer shares of their business to the public in a new stock issuance. Public share issuance allows a company to raise capital from public investors. Industry giants, such as Google and Meta, raised billions in capital through IPOs. In 2021, Nykaa entered this big league of IPO in India's stock market.

Pros: No obligation to repay the money. No additional financial burden on the company.

Cons: A percentage of your company goes to the investors. The startup has to share the profit and consult with investors while making decisions.

2. Debt Financing: This process involves borrowing money and paying it back with interest. Debt financing occurs when a startup raises money for its capital expenditures by selling debt instruments to individuals and/or institutional investors. In such a scenario, the investors become creditors and receive a promise that the principal and interest on the debt will be repaid. Companies that sell fixed income products—such as bonds, bills, or notes—to investors to obtain the capital needed for the growth and expansion of their operations choose debt financing. Retail or institutional investors are the lenders who provide the company with debt financing. The amount of the investment loan, also known as the principal, must be paid back at some agreed date in the future. If the company goes bankrupt, lenders can lay claim to any liquidated assets.

Some investors in debt are only interested in principal protection, while others take a return in the form of interest. The rate of interest is determined by market rates and the creditworthiness of the borrower. A greater chance of default draws a higher rate of interest and thus, carries a higher level of risk. Debt financing often requires the borrower to adhere to certain rules called covenants regarding financial performance.

Sources of debt financing: Banks, Non-Banking Financial Institutions, and Government Loan Schemes.

Pros: It allows a business to leverage a small amount of capital to create growth and is generally tax-deductible. The company retains all ownership control.

Cons: The startup must pay the interest, which is regardless of business revenue. This type of financing is unsuitable for businesses with inconsistent cash flow.

Is Equity Better Than Debt Financing: Although in equity financing the money need not be repaid, the funding process has some drawbacks. The startup company must generate consistent profits to maintain a healthy stock valuation and pay dividends to its shareholders.

Since equity financing is a greater risk to the investor than debt financing is to the lender, the cost of equity is often higher than the cost of debt. Any smart business strategy will include a consideration of the balance between debt and equity financing that is the most cost-effective.

3. Grants: A financial award that is given by an entity to a company to facilitate a goal or incentivize performance is termed Grants. There is no component of repayment of the invested funds. There is a risk of the startup not meeting the goal or objective for which the grant has been provided. Grants are distributed in different tranches with respect to the fulfillment of the corresponding milestone. Thus, a startup is constantly working to achieve the milestones laid down. There is no return and no involvement in decision-making for the provider of the grants.

Sources of grants: Central Government Grants, State Government Grants, Corporate Challenges, Grant Programs of Private Entities.

Sources of Funding

Starting a startup is not a cakewalk and is not for the faint-hearted because it does not happen overnight.

From the steps of ideation to the milestone of profit making, there are several hurdles to face and overcome. Fundraising comes as the third step, much later to ideation and company formation. Fundraising is a crucial and intense process and the founders must become well-versed with terms like venture debt, convertible notes, liquidation preference, anti-dilution protection, and drag-along rights. Investors cannot put their money into a business whose founder is naïve to such terminologies. As the startup goes through different phases, investors may develop different objectives and methods in successive rounds of funding. Broadly, funds for a startup can be obtained through seven sources.

1. **Friends and family:** The most common form of funding as well as being one of the safest and the most reliable ways of funding as the lenders know you enough to put their trust in you. Besides, you always have them by your side.
2. **Crowdfunding:** It is opted by a number of startups these days. There are certain websites that are dedicated to collecting investments from a host of investors and helping budding startups in setting up their businesses. Setting up a crowdfunding campaign is not very difficult.

    You set up a profile on a crowdfunding site, describing your company and its business, and the amount of money you are trying to raise. People who are interested in what you are trying to do can donate to your campaign, typically in exchange for some kind of reward for their donation (one of your products or services, a discount based on how much donated, or some other perk), or for some form of equity or profit share in your business.

    The key to successful crowdfunding campaigns is to have a compelling story about your product and to offer a meaningful reward for donations. Rewards-based crowdfunding is a particularly attractive option for startups, as you are not giving away equity or part ownership in your company.

But you will be offering some of your products or services, or a discount on those products or services. And reward-based campaigns are not burdened with interest or principal repayments the way small business loans are. A crowdfunding campaign can also work to build a community of people interested in your company or products, and provides a sense of engagement for the donor. On the same note, equity crowdfunding is a little complex as you are selling stock or some other interest in your company in exchange for cash. You must get in touch with legal services and comply with the rules and regulations.

3. **Government loan schemes:** As startups are gaining momentum due to their ability to create jobs, government schemes provide collateral-free debt to aspiring startups and facilitate access to low-cost capital.
4. **Grants:** This type of funding typically applies to businesses operating in the research and development process. Grants are offered by the government because most of these startups are run and regulated by the government itself.
5. **Business incubators:** They are specially designed programs to help young startups innovate and grow. They usually provide workspaces, mentorship, education, and access to investors for startups or sole entrepreneurs. These resources allow companies and ideas to prosper while operating at a lower cost during the early stages of business incubation.

    Incubators require an application process to join and usually require a commitment for a specific amount of time. Incubators typically follow a less rigid schedule and can be tailored to a business's unique needs. These programs are like residencies with the added benefit of educational programming and mentorship. Generally, you can stay in an incubator for as long as it takes you to grow your business to a sustainable level.

6. **Angel investors:** At the nascent stage of your business, you have to look for angel investors. They just listen to your pitch and invest in your idea when they foresee a promising association. Investment is not very huge and they do not get into the technicality of the business. Angel investors care about the quality, passion, commitment, and integrity of the founders. They check on the market opportunity and the potential for the company to become very big. Although not inclined much toward the technicality, they indeed look for the business plan and seek out the evidence of obtaining traction toward the plan. Angel investors are often keen on anything that can lead to intellectual property rights. And they check on the viability of raising additional rounds of startup funding if progress is made. Angel investors are much more likely to invest if they know your sector well; so, it often helps to start with your connections in that sector. Serial entrepreneurs with successful past liquidity events are often some of the best angel investors. They come with the cash and also bring in additional benefits like contacts to strategic partners and venture capitalists, credibility, and contacts to potential customers and employees.

7. **Venture Capitalists:** They lend money only upon liking a business model and after contemplating its prospects. Usually, they invest a lump sum and do expect high returns. Venture Capitalist (VC) firms can provide capital; strategic assistance; introductions to potential customers, partners, and employees; and much more. However, VC financing is not easy to obtain. VCs typically want to invest in startups that are pursuing big opportunities with high growth potential and have already shown some traction.

They prefer startups that have a working product prototype, early customer adoption, etc. It is important to know that venture capitalists typically focus their investment efforts after checking their alignment with specific industry sectors (software, semiconductor, SaaS, biotech, mobile devices, etc.) and the stage of the company—early-stage seed or Series A rounds, or later stage rounds with companies that have achieved meaningful revenues and traction. The best way to get the attention of a VC firm is to have a warm introduction through one of their trusted colleagues, or another professional acquaintance of the firm, such as a lawyer or fellow entrepreneur.

The venture process is time consuming and the key terms negotiated in a venture financing deal include the following:

- Valuation of the company and the amount and form of the investment (typically through convertible preferred stock).
- Liquidation preference of the equity investment.
- Board of Directors composition and any Board observer rights.
- Approval or "veto" rights of the investors for future equity financings, sale of the company, or changes to charter documents.
- Preemptive rights and rights to receive periodic financial reports and other information, insurance obligations, etc.
- Anti-dilution protection in case the future rounds of financing occur at a reduced valuation.
- Venture capital financing can be crucial to the success of a startup. Entrepreneurs must understand the key issues in venture financing, which can further increase the likelihood of a successful outcome.

In the end, it is imperative for every entrepreneur to scrutinize the pros and cons of their idea before they lay it on the ground. Good funding will help a startup go a long way without losing balance. As the first search begins with angel investors, let us find out what an angel investor looks for in a startup before investing.

The Key Features Of Angel Investment

Experienced angel investors are meticulous in reviewing investment proposals. Every investor has certain boxes to check before they take interest in your project, inject money, or give their time to a startup.

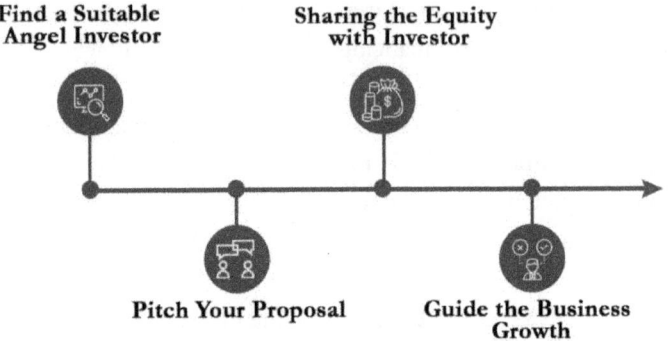

This is a simple pictorial representation of how angel investment works. Now, let us have a look at what these investors need before making an investment in a venture.

How dynamic is your market? This is the first question where an investor wishes to know how big your market is, both in the present and after future expansion. If you are targeting an existing market, be prepared to answer how your offerings are different from that of the other players. If it is an emerging market, focus on answering how big the market is expected to grow in the next few years and the growth drivers. Remember, angel investors are ready to test new waters.

How abled is your team? A seasoned investor will be keen to know how well your team is positioned to create and execute the business idea and become the market leader.

They do check if your core team has domain expertise. The chemistry between the team members and their competency are going to come under thorough scrutiny. Basically, angel investors repose their faith in the jockey and not in the horse. Remember, the business idea may swivel over time while the team is responsible for success.

What is your commercial traction? Commercial traction gives you an upper hand over your competitors. Having real data to support your claims allows you to adjust the assumptions you started with. For an angel investor, it is a good measure of your progress. The data proves that the market is already engaged with your product and thus investors can have faith in your company.

How fit is your investor? Investor-fit is one of the most important parameters for an entrepreneur to consider while opting for an angel investor. The investor must be on the same page as you. Do your research before approaching them. This way, you will remove the ones from your list who are not a good fit.

Do you have the X-factor? There is always a click moment between the investor and the founder that affects the investment decision. Sometimes it is as simple as affinity, based on the shared workplace, a common background, the same alma mater, or a mutually trusted and known connection. And sometimes it is just a gut feeling. Get to know the background of the investor and present yourself in the best way possible. Realize that fundraising is difficult. You WILL NOT get the checks immediately, so do your homework well in time.

Is Bootstrapping Out Of Fashion?

While we chalk out the nitty-gritty of funding sources, does bootstrapping remain a long-lost dream? A startup is about the challenge of making something out of nothing.

The term 'bootstrapping' was used during the 18th and 19th centuries to refer to an impossible task. In the world of business, the terms 'bootstrapping' and 'bootstrapped business' refer to businesses that are built using only existing resources, such as personal savings, personal computing equipment, and garage space, to start and grow a company. Bootstrapping signifies a funding situation in which an entrepreneur starts a company with little capital, relying on his/her money other than on any outside investments. Bootstrapping often relates to a procedure used to calculate the zero-coupon yield curve from market figures. Bootstrapped entrepreneurs rely on personal savings, sweat equity, lean operations, quick inventory turnover, and a cash runway to become successful. For example, a bootstrapped company often takes preorders for its product and uses the funds generated from the orders to build and deliver the product itself.

"As long as you can bootstrap, not at the sacrifice of competitive advantage, bootstrapping is a really powerful thing because it allows you to be totally devoted to your vision."
–Nick Woodman

Case Study: The ZOHO Way

One of the oldest bootstrapped companies in India is Zoho. It was founded nearly 25 years ago by Sridhar Vembu and today it is one of the biggest SaaS companies. It deals in an array of services, such as software development, Web hosting, email hosting, and cloud computing; it also offers web-based business tools, such as database, spreadsheets, web conferencing, note takings, customer relationship management, and wikis, to other companies. The early 2000s witnessed the advent of the dot com bubble and Zoho did go through a period of losing some of its customers. Nevertheless, Zoho survived since they were debt-free. The company did not have any major liabilities that had to be paid on a continuous basis, and thus Zoho was able to regroup and ride out the difficult time.

Though many entrepreneurs entered the IPO club, Zoho has remained private, and thus it does not have to worry about disclosures, public scandals, securities laws, and other factors that can choke out even the most promising companies. Zoho is accountable only to the Vembu family: they founded the company and continue to manage its day-to-day operations.

If finding inspiration is becoming difficult for young entrepreneurs, the fascinating story of Sridhar Vembu and Zoho's success can be your destination. Bootstrappers take an idea, and then use their talent and professionalism to build a worthwhile business. It indeed takes great dedication, sound work ethics, and pure single-mindedness to achieve success this way.

Bootstrapping utilizes the following options:

- Owner Financing and Personal Debt.
- Sweat Equity—the founder's contribution to the company in the form of effort.
- Keeping the operating costs low and the inventory minimized.
- Subsidy Finance—government cash payments or tax reductions.
- Securing cash to run the business that comes from sales.
- A bootstrap company can be successful if the entrepreneur executes a big idea, focuses on profits, develops skills, and becomes a better business person.

Growth of a Bootstrapped Company

A bootstrapped company usually grows through three successive funding stages:
- Beginning Stage: The founder continues to work a day job and starts the business on the side. The business is started with some personal savings, debt, or investment money from friends and family.

> Customer-Funded Stage: In this stage, money from the customers is used to keep the business in operation and eventually, fund its growth.
> Credit Stage: At this stage, the entrepreneur focuses on the funding of specific activities, such as improving equipment and hiring staff. The company takes out loans or may even find venture capital, for expansion.

Bootstrapping is not out of fashion. Many early-stage companies that do not require large inflows of capital and have the flexibility and time to grow opt for bootstrapping. Similarly, serial entrepreneur companies, where the founder has money from the sale of a previous company to invest, often bootstrap.

Advantages	Disadvantages
Cheap with low cost of entry.	Problems with the cash flow.
You are your own boss	Equity issues arise if there are multiple founders.
You have the freedom and flexibility to develop your business.	Risk of failure is high and thus stress is more.

Many successful companies of the world had a humble beginning through bootstrapping. Dell Computers, Apple, Microsoft, and Meta (Facebook) were all bootstrap enterprises. Bootstrapping continues to be an attractive option for startup entrepreneurs. You have to keep a balance between the benefits and the risks and plan ahead to see the scope of bringing in outside money.

Case Study: The Success Story Of Zerodha

Zerodha was founded in 2010 with a team of merely five people when the Kamath brothers began their entrepreneurship journey the old-school way. The company name has a significant connotation: it is said to be a blend of the English word 'zero' and the Sanskrit word 'rodha,' which means barrier. True to its name, Zerodha has literally made trading a barrier-free activity. Presently, Zerodha has more than 1,200 employees and 1.9 lakh users. Blending a unique idea with technology, the Kamath brothers have taken the online discount broking company to earn 120 crore INR as revenue in the FY20-21. They brought the first twist of success in December 2015, when Zerodha became the first Indian brokerage firm to go completely brokerage-free for equity investments.

Zerodha is a member of NSE, BSE, MCX, and MCX-SX, and provides brokerage services to stock market traders. The feature that sets Zerodha apart from the other startups is Nithin Kamath's decision to steer clear of outside money. From the beginning, when Nithin was a sub-broker with Reliance and was also involved in providing portfolio advisory services, he never appreciated the obligation of being answerable for someone else's money.

Zerodha works on a 'low margin–high volume' business model and operates on the B2B format. It charges a negligible amount to the dealers for transactions because of which the exchanging volume is normally high. It does not have a straightforward revenue model. However, the company is arguably one of the most used trading networks in India and has made headlines on earning a $1 billion valuation without any outside investors. Zerodha is now valued at a whopping $3 billion in the Hurun Global Unicorn List of 2020 and has initiated funds and incubated the innovative Indian fintech startup named Rainmatter. To date, Rainmatter has made 11 investments, of which 7 are lead investments, and their most recent investment was made on January 28, 2021, when GrowFix raised $2 million.

A few decades earlier, the first-generation entrepreneurs did choose to go for VCs, angel investors, government funds, and even debt funds, banks, and NBFCs. However, times are changing and new age startups have realized that equity money is not free money. Even today, a large number of startups remain dependent on external funding for survival and growth.

Nevertheless, there are founders who still believe in maintaining a complete stake in the company and growing organically for survival. Mudraka, HappyFox, and Gxpress are some of the bootstrap startups that are writing their success stories.

"I could have raised external funds but as I said, this whole obligation of picking up a phone call any time of the day to answer is something that I did not want to go through."
–Nithin Kamath

In India, choosing business as a career is itself a dilemma, and then deciding to scale it further without any external fundraising is certainly one of the toughest decisions. The success stories of these bootstrap startups may change the market sentiment altogether in India.

Funding At Different Stages Of Startup

As stated earlier, a startup goes through several stages and each stage is entitled to have different sources of funding. Let us have a look at how startups can utilize the different funding options.

Ideation Stage: It is the initial stage of the business where only a small amount of funds is needed. Additionally, there are limited and mostly informal channels available for raising funds. It is often called the pre-seed stage and there are mainly three options available.

- **Bootstrapping:** This is the first recourse for most entrepreneurs as there is no pressure to pay back the funds or dilute control of your startup.
- **Friends and Family:** The trust level is inherent between the entrepreneurs and the investors.
- **Pitching Event:** It includes the financial benefits that are provided by institutes or organizations that conduct business plan competitions and challenges. The amount of money is not large but is usually enough at the idea stage.

At this stage, a startup has a prototype ready and needs to validate the potential demand for the startup's product/service. The startup conducts a Proof of Concept (POC) and then proceeds to the big market launch.

Seed Stage: At this stage the startup conducts field trials, tests the product on a few potential customers, onboard mentors, and builds a formal team. At this stage, it can explore the following options:

- **Incubators:** They offer a lot of value-added services like office space, utilities, and admin and legal assistance and they often make grants/debt/equity investments as well.
- **Government Loan Schemes:** This is to provide collateral-free debt to aspiring entrepreneurs and help them gain access to low-cost capital. Example: Startup India Seed Fund Scheme and SIDBI Fund of Funds.
- Angel Investors.
- Crowdfunding.

Early Traction Stage: This is the stage when the startup's products or services have been launched in the market. Key performance indicators such as customer base, revenue, and app downloads are some of the important credentials at this stage. This is called the Series A Stage and funds are raised at this stage to further grow the user base, increase the product offerings, expand to new geographies, etc. Common funding sources utilized by startups in this stage are listed below:

- **Venture Capital Funds:** VCs take startup equity in return for their investments and actively engage in the mentorship of their investee startups.
- **Banks/Non-Banking Financial Companies (NBFCs):** Formal debt can be raised from banks and NBFCs at this stage as the startup can show market traction and revenue to validate its ability to finance interest payment obligations. Some entrepreneurs might prefer debt over equity as debt

funding does not dilute equity stake.
- **Venture Debt Funds:** They are private investment funds that invest money in startups primarily in the form of debt. Debt funds typically invest along with an angel or VC round.

Scaling stage: A stage of market growth and increasing revenues is called the scaling stage. At this stage the funding is called Series B, C, D, and E, and some of the common sources are as follows:
- **Venture Capital Funds:** At this late stage of the startup, VCs come with larger ticket sizes in their investment thesis. It is recommended to approach these funds only after the startup has generated significant market traction. Sometimes, a pool of VCs come together and fund a startup as well.
- **Private Equity/Investment Firms:** Though it is unusual, lately some private equity and investment firms have been providing funds for fast-growing late-stage startups who have maintained a consistent growth record.

Exit Options: A startup can opt for different exit options.
- **Mergers and Acquisitions:** In this case, the investor may decide to sell the portfolio company to another company in the market. Essentially, it is about one company combining with another, either by acquiring it in full or in part or by being acquired (whole or in part). Example: Akash Educational Services and Byju's went for a merger, while Tata Digital acquired the majority stake in Bigbasket.
- **Initial Public Offering (IPO):** It is an option for a startup to list on the stock market for the first time. Since the public listing process is elaborate and consists of statutory formalities, it is generally undertaken by startups with an impressive track record of profits and who are growing at a steady pace. Examples: Zomato, CarTrade, Paytm, Nykaa, and MapmyIndia.

- **Selling Shares:** Investors can sell their equity or shares to other venture capital or private equity firms.
- **Buybacks:** If the founders of the startup have liquid assets, they may also buy back their shares from the fund/investors and regain control of their company.
- **Distressed Sale:** During financially stressful times for a startup company, the investors may decide to sell the business to another company or financial institution.

A Hypothetical Startup Case Study

Let us make a case scenario of you setting up your startup.

Stage 1- Hatching the Idea

You have conceived a brilliant idea to start with. Right from the day you start working, you create value. At a later stage, this value is going to be translated into equity. But right now, you own everything in your unregistered company, so you need not think of equity now.

Stage 2 – Finding the Right Cofounder

Once you start making your idea into a physical prototype, you realize the need for someone else in the team. Soon, you find someone who is equally enthusiastic toward your idea and is smart enough to add value. You make them an offer to become a cofounder because you do not wish to pay them like an employee. Instead, you offer sweat equity, that is, equity in exchange for their valuable contribution in building your startup. But how much should you give? A 20 percent equity would be considered too little, while you cannot afford to give a 40 percent equity. However, considering the amount of faith the cofounder is putting into your idea, you decide to share 50 percent. This adjustment ensures trust and also motivates the cofounder. All said and done, you need external funding as your startup starts growing. Your heart prefers to go to a VC, but then you do not have a working product with which to pitch your business well.

Stage 3 – Family and Friends Funding Round

You wish to put an ad in the newspapers seeking money from outsiders, but soon you realize that you are legally bound. The general public will not invest in a small private startup. So, you are now left with two options:

- **Accredited investors** – This can be anyone in your circle who either has Rs 5 crore in the bank or makes Rs 50 lakh annually. They are usually sophisticated investors who are held in high esteem, with enough capacity to decide whether to invest in an ultra-risky company like yours.
- **Family and Friends** – What if your cofounder has a rich Uncle? You give him five percent of the company in exchange for Rs 15 lakh. Now you can afford enough resources for six months while building your prototype. Presently, let us say you value your company at Rs 3 crore.

Stage 4 – Register the company

You register your company to give Uncle the five percent. You issue some common stock, give five percent to Uncle, and set aside 20 percent for your future employees – that is the option pool. Why? Because your future investor will want an option pool. And secondly, the stock remains safe from you and your cofounders doing anything with it.

Stage 5 – Angel Round

Uncle's cash is fast burning out and soon you realize that you need to start looking for your next startup funding source. What options do you have now?

- **Incubators, accelerators, and excubators** – They will provide cash, working space, and advisors. The cash amount is about Rs 50 to 70 lakh (for 5%–10% of the company.) Some advisors are better than cash, like Unicorns or successful businessmen who want to enter the startup arena.

> **Angel investors** – They often lend from Rs 1.5 crore to Rs 2 crore, but they give this amount to companies that value around Rs 7 crore to Rs 10 crore. Make the best pitch possible ever. You find an angel who looks at your still-in-process prototype and thinks that it is worth Rs 5 crore. He agrees to invest Rs 75 lakh to Rs 1 crore.

In this case, let us understand what percentage of the company you should give to the angel investor. NOT 20 percent. We have to add the 'pre-money valuation,' which is the company's worth before new money and further investment come in.

Rs 5 crore + Rs 1 crore = Rs 6 crore: this is your post-money valuation

You have to think in this way: first you take the money, then you give the shares. If you give the shares before you add the angel's investment, you will end up dividing what was there before the angel joined. Now divide the investment by the post-money valuation, i.e., 1 Cr/6 Cr. It comes around 16.7 percent and that is what the angel investor gets.

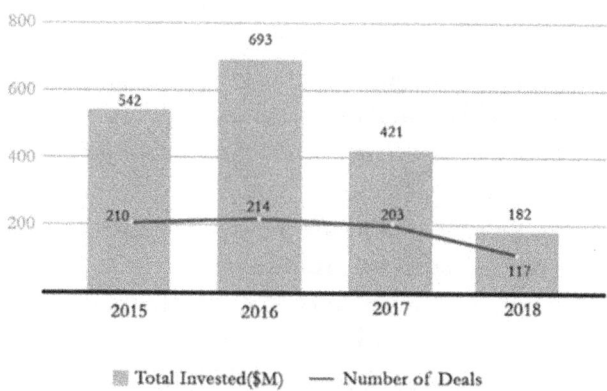

Angel Investment Scenario In India

There is a reason why they are called angel investors. They bring in the difference before a startup burns to death. It is crucial to have the initial fund injection by an investor. They carry the ability to validate the business model, build a pilot, and connect with the first customer, which are essential steps for any budding entrepreneur.

Stage 6 – Venture Capital Round

In this stage, you have built your first version and you have traction with the users. You are now ready to approach VCs who invest above Rs 3 crore to Rs 5 crore. Let us assume that the VC values your present worth at Rs 25 crore. Again, that is your pre-money valuation and he is willing to invest Rs 7 crore. Putting the same mathematical logic here, the VC gets 22 percent of your company. Now, your company is the VC's company too.

Your first VC round is your series A. Now you can go on to have series B and C, which occur at different points in time. There are two possibilities: either no one shows interest in investing in your company and it shuts down or you build something so good that a bigger organization wishes to buy/acquire you. Apart from this, there is another chance that your company does so well that you wish to go public.

Now, you are at a stage when you have secured enough funding for your startup. You can take the product to newer markets, sign up more customers, hire for key positions, and scale operations. The money you just landed will provide some immediate boost, but money alone will not be enough to make it as big as you are dreaming of. You will need solid backing from your investors, who can help you with new introductions, promotion, and advice on various aspects of running a successful business. Engage them, build trust, and strengthen relationships. Investors love it when they are acknowledged and sought after. They would always wish to know the fate of their investment. Additionally, at this stage tracking and reporting on the right metrics come into the scene. While sending monthly updates to the investor is a good option, it may become too much for a very early-stage startup.

ENTREPRENEURSHIP EPIDEMIC

You can work out the reporting frequency with your investor. Similarly, depending on the stage of the startup, company size, revenue, and future funding requirements, you should plan out your metrics.

HOW STARTUP FUNDING WORKS
A Hypothetical Startup Going From Idea To IPO

money raised

| How much you get | | | | | | | IPO (Initial Public Offering) |

₹650 Cr. ₹8122 Cr. Valuation (Unicorn)

100% OF NOTHING   IS A LOT LESS THAN   17% OF A BIG COMPANY...   SERIES C / SERIES B

₹7 Cr.   ₹25 Cr. Valuation   SERIES A

₹1 Cr.   ₹6 Cr. Valuation   SEED ROUND

₹15 Lakhs (₹3 Cr. Valuation)   FAMILY & FRIENDS

How do you get it: IDEA STAGE / CO-FOUNDER STAGE

Some more series of funding

What you give

- Founder: 100%
- Founder 1: 37.5%, Founder 2: 37.5%, uncle 5%, option pool 20%
- Founder 1: 31.2%, Founder 2: 31.2%, uncle (option pool?) — Stock set aside for future employees
- Founder 1: 13.5%, Founder 2: 19.2%, uncle 2.8%, option pool 16.1%, Angel, VC 33.3%
- Founder 1: 17.6%, Founder 2: 17.6%, uncle 2.4%, option pool 12.5%, angel 5.5%, first employee 1.7%, VC 30.5%, Public

Founder 1 / Founder 2 — 50% / 50%

What everyone does

YOU	CO-FOUNDER	FRIENDS & FAMILY	ANGEL INVESTORS	VENTURE CAPITALISTS	EARLY EMPLOYEES	INVESTMENT BANKERS	ANYONE
Start The Company	Shares half of the work	Invests before anymore else at the lowest price.	Has at least ₹5 Cr. in Bank or makes ₹50 lakhs annually- is on accredited investor list. Invests Their Money	Persuades other people to put money in his fund, invests that money, starting ₹7 Cr.	Gamble on your company by accepting low salary plus some stock	Does IPO paperwork and sells a lot of your stock, getting 3 to 7% of the whole IPO for it.	After your company does the IPO, anyone in the world can become your investor.

Now, look at the key performance indicators and metrics to keep your next series of funding free of doubts.

Revenue Against Goal: Absolute revenue number is just a data point. Connect the data points and establish trends by providing context, such as revenue against goal, average revenue, percentage revenue growth, revenue against forecast, and comparison with the previous period. Let us have a look at the simplest way of calculating the requirements.

- *Average Revenue: Total revenue amassed/No. of months.*
- *% Revenue Growth = [(Revenue in this month - Revenue in previous month)/Revenue in previous month] × 100*
- *Revenue overachieved or underachieved = actual revenue - forecast revenue*
- *Revenue comparison of this year versus last year: Comparison of revenue with the previous period offers context and shows increase/decrease over the last year.*
- *% Revenue from new customers = [revenue from new customers (revenue from existing customers + revenue from new customers)] × 100*
- *Average revenue per user = Total operating revenue/Number of users*
- *Monthly recurring revenue (MRR): Net MRR = new MRR + expansion MRR – lost MRR*

Gross and Net Burn: Gross Burn is the amount of cash a company is spending each month, while Net Burn is the amount of money a company is losing each month.

Cash on hand and months of runway: You have to update investors about how much cash you are left with and how many months it will last. This gives them a clear idea of timelines to kickstart the next fundraising. By this process they will be aware of the amount of capital they should keep it available.

They will also introduce you to other potential investors for the next funding round. You can calculate the same with the following formula:

- Months of runway = Cash in bank / Burn rate

Number of Users: You have to update the investors about the number of users, both actual users and forecasted users.

Percentage paying users = (Number of paying users / Total number of users) X 100

- % New customers acquired = [No. of new customers / (No. of existing customers + No. of new customers)] X 100
- Net customers = Existing customer base + renewals + new customers – cancellations

Churn rate: Customer churn rate is the percentage of total customers who chose to cancel their subscriptions during the period.

- Churn rate = (Number of customers lost / total number of customers) X 100

Updating your investors is more than professionalism. It is about ensuring that the trust remains. Proactive, consistent, and professional investor updates are never an obligation or responsibility but an opportunity to show that you are diligent, accountable, and transparent in your business endeavor. Always remember that investors prefer visual updates with data-driven charts and minimum text. Charts make it easy to process and absorb data, spot trends, and see the bigger picture.

When Can You Go for IPO?

IPO is just another way to raise money while the source varies. It is not from a VC firm or an angel investor but from millions of regular people. Through an IPO, a company can sell stocks on the stock market and anyone can buy them.

Since anyone can buy, you can sell a lot of stock right away rather than go to individual investors and ask them to invest. Although it sounds easier to acquire funds through this method, your company must have attained that much reputation in the market to have joined the bandwagon. On the same note, IPO opens another avenue for consideration. All those people who have invested in your company so far, including you, are holding the restricted stock basically, which you cannot simply go and sell for cash. Restricted stocks are not verified by the government. Unless the government sees your IPO paperwork, you might as well be selling some unusual herbs, for all people know. The government has to make sure that your product is genuine before it lets regular people invest in your company.

Now, all those who have invested in your company so far would finally like to convert or sell their restricted stock and get cash or unrestricted stock. The latter is almost as good as cash. This stage is called the liquidity event. Moreover, there is another group of people who would really urge you to go for an IPO. These are the investment bankers, such as HDFC Bank, Axis Bank, JM Financials, and Morgan Stanley. They often wish to be your lead underwriters by preparing your IPO paperwork and calling up wealthy clients to sell them your stock. These bankers get three percent to seven percent of all the money you raise in the IPO.

The primary benefit of going public via an IPO is the ability to raise capital quickly by reaching a large number of investors. A company can use that cash to further the business, be it in the form of research, infrastructure, or expansion. Additionally, by issuing shares, newer, lesser-known companies can generate publicity and increase their business opportunities. Moreover, there is indeed an added prestige to being listed on a major stock exchange. IPOs can help growing companies attract new talent by offering perks like stock options. One major drawback of going public using an IPO is the time and expense of going through the process. It may take you anywhere from six to nine months or longer. And if your management team is completely focused on the IPO, other areas of the business will suffer.

More than anything, it costs money to go through with an IPO, from financial service and underwriting fees to filing fees. And once a company goes public, it becomes subject to a host of additional reporting and disclosure requirements.

Furthermore, once a company goes public, it must answer to its shareholders. As they gain a significant ownership stake in a company, they can vote to override management decisions, or vote to get rid of managers and directors altogether. So, before you jump the gun, you must realize that going the IPO way will pressurize you to perform well for the shareholders. Undue pressure often leads to poor business decisions, while sacrificing long-term growth for short-term profits. Thus, evaluate both the benefits and the drawbacks before you file for IPO.

How Much Money Do You Actually Need?

The influx of money certainly creates room for growth. But, do you know how much money your startup actually needs? As a startup founder, your ownership should be your prime concern as early money is the most expensive money. Look at the strings attached before you chalk out a long-term equity dilution. For many entrepreneurs, a successful fundraising round is a time to celebrate; however, it is also a crucial step to reflect and retrospect. The funding comes at the expense of control and room to maneuver later on. Figuring out how much is actually needed is quite difficult as the market of entrepreneurship is quite volatile. If you raise too much, you end up giving away an unduly large portion of your company and if you raise too little, you risk running out of cash before you achieve the target. Meanwhile, understanding the ins and outs of various financing instruments and their long-term implications is intimidating.

Entrepreneurs raise three key questions while decking up on their fund-raising pitch: How much money to raise? What percentage of the company should be sold? What company valuation should be used?

These three questions are mathematically intertwined and there are two approaches entrepreneurs can take. Either they decide on how much money is needed and move forward or they decide on how much of the company they wish to sell and work it backward.

In the first approach of raising the fund, some advisors urge to raise as much as you can. VCs and investors will usually ask startups to raise enough to last 12 to 18 months before they need to raise money again.

Regarding the second approach of selling the company, the general rule of thumb for angel/seed stage rounds is that founders should **sell between 10 percent and 20 percent of the equity** in the company. How could anyone conclude that? The assumption is based on what an early equity investor looks for in terms of return. They place bets on the startup with the clear knowledge that most of their investments will give zero return. They are exposed to a high-risk and high-potential scenario; thus, they would want a decent slice of equity to get a meaningful return if things go well, and also to have a meaningful level of influence and control of key company decisions if they do not.

So, how do you value the startup? The biggest determinants of your startup's value are the market forces of the industry and sector you have chosen: the balance between demand and supply of money, the size of recent exits, the willingness for an investor to pay a premium to get into a deal, and the level of your desperation while looking for money. Sooner or later, it boils down to the entrepreneur's gut feeling, profit ensuring efforts, and art of pitching the proposal. Still there are some loopholes every entrepreneur should look at.

> ➢ **Increasing investments NEVER ensures success of a startup.** The central banks have released a global glut of liquidity and money is no more a difficult task to raise amidst the COVID-19 pandemic.
>
> The millions being invested in startups speaks about the large bets on distant outcomes, and not value generation by way of revenues.

No one can assume the high rate of survival of these startups with such investments. Investment is not equal to profit. The success of a business lies in a thousand other operational aspects.

- **There prevails a gap in the sectors chosen.** One can see this as a hurdle or a new avenue to encroach when India remains a marginal player in the space startup sector. India is mainly focused on fintech and eCommerce, which leaves a huge gap in the space sector to fill or compete in or a scope to progress. Currently, the global space economy is worth $440 billion, with India having less than a two percent share in the sector. It is a little surprising as India is a leading space-faring country with end-to-end capabilities to make satellites, develop augmented launch vehicles, and deploy interplanetary missions. However, the problem lies in the lack of independent private participation in the space sector due to the absence of a framework to provide transparency and clarity in the associated laws.

- **Risk-aversion is common.** Do you know that the big investors in India's startup sector are from overseas? The SoftBank Group is a Japanese multinational conglomerate, the Alibaba Group is a Chinese multinational tech company, and Sequoia Capital is an American venture capital firm. India lacks a serious VC industry with an appetite for risk. The country's established conglomerates have mostly stuck to traditional businesses, although there is a change now with many conglomerates joining in the pursuit of some of the fast-growing startup sectors.

Invariably, every step of business revolves around the art of communication. Business proposals must be sold well. If you are capable of building a business pitch that can bowl out your customers as well as investors, you know the game.

If you fail to communicate well, then no matter how great your business idea is, you will fall short in raising funds and securing a place in the market; you will also fail to capture your customers' attention. Whether to allure investors or to increase your customer base, you have to indulge in the art of storytelling.

"Fundraising is sales. Marketing is sales at scale. Sales is the #1 skill for any startup. Bootstrapped or VCs."—Jesse Pujji

Startups Need Powerful Storytelling

Any business that wishes to build a powerful and lasting brand must understand the significance of storytelling. It is an art and an essential ingredient of day-to-day communication. If done well, storytelling can do wonders for your brand and business. Storytelling highlights your purpose, and businesses with purpose are the ones that ultimately stand out and capture the consumer's hearts and wallets. A startup gathers several benefits by incorporating a strategic storytelling practice.

> ➢ **Strong Marketing Strategy:** A well-communicated story about your business's mission, vision, and product forms the backbone of your marketing strategy. A clear, captivating, and effective story around your product forms the first selling pitch. Stories create a blueprint of your business idea. When a brand's marketing strategy is created around a story, the content describes the intention and value proposition of the business and also supports the business' overarching vision.

> ➢ **Imparting a Human Touch:** Customers like the idea of investing in people more than just investing in an inanimate company or business. Some of the most admired and financially successful companies are known not only for delivering financial returns. It is both an ethical and strategic move for businesses to humanize their brand and purpose.

- ➤ Imparts a Competitive Advantage: Your startup can have a better product than that of a competitor, but most often, customers make their decisions based on emotion rather than logic. The ability to tell a good story is essential and can make or break how well a business differentiates itself in the market and makes a profit.
- ➤ Create Brand Loyalty: Stories allow your brand to connect with the customers emotionally and thus help in creating brand loyalty. A business that talks about success, struggles, conflicts, and setbacks is considered more real by the customers.

Powerful storytelling invokes an emotional response from the customers. Target the heart and not the head. Consider the core values of your business and bring them out with a story that pulls in the reader with a simple, personal, and meaningful arc that cannot be forgotten easily. Making your brand story relatable to your customers is important; thus, a startup should focus on how the product or service can eliminate negatives, reinforce positives, and help the customer move. An engaging storyline makes the potential customers inquisitive toward your product.

Have you watched the trending advertisement of Akash-Byju's? They are infusing the edtech sector into the customers' minds while chalking out the emotional bond between teachers and students. Similarly, using satire and fun is another way to allure customers. One of the best examples is the CRED ad with cricketers. The idea is to make your customer/investor ruminate upon something interesting.

Storytelling and testimonials are crucial for any business to grow. They provide free publicity and create awareness among verticals, and a well-told success story can make the difference between a sale and a wasted call. Your narrative must bear the elements of sincerity. As a startup, you may not have a success story yet; nevertheless, you can always have an insight story.

Whether you are targeting your customers or trying to pitch your idea to secure funds, you need a compelling storyline to make people believe in your efforts.

So, how do you make effective storytelling for your startup? Here are some of the crucial tips:

- ➢ Draw on real-life experiences and give a human touch.
- ➢ Narrate how your product is standing ahead of the competition.
- ➢ Appeal to people's lifestyles and problems and provide your solution.
- ➢ Make the content digestible and acceptable.
- ➢ Include teasers to invoke interest.

The present business arena is fast-paced and is conducive to the social marketing environment. Storytelling has become an essential part of crafting valuable engagement with the consumers to improve sales and attract investors. It is no longer an underrated skill in business, but once a story is well-crafted and well-told, it becomes a tool to raise money, recruit talent, and attract customers. It can also be the thing that keeps your startup's mission forever in the forefront.

"The best entrepreneurs are not the best visionaries. The greatest entrepreneurs are incredible salespeople. They know how to tell an amazing story that will convince talent and investors to join in on the journey."

— Alejandro Cremades

Key Takeaways:

- Learn about how to fund your startup
- Why do startups need the power of storytelling?
- Funding sources at different stages of a startup

7

STARTUP: BEING THE BOSS IS NOT EASY

Sleepless nights, anxiety, loneliness, unforeseen expenses, and whatnot. Startup success stories that make the rounds in numerous blogs or websites hardly acknowledge the dark side of the business. The back-breaking hard work, intense focus, personal and professional sacrifices, and the cost of opportunity at every stage are never mentioned. Building a startup brings along ridicule and unavoidable pain, and of course, a great risk of failure. Retention of the business, revenue generation, and keeping up with the market make up the soul of a startup, without which it cannot survive.

> *"No more romanticizing about how cool it is to be an entrepreneur. It's a struggle to save your company's life—and your own skin—every day of the week."* – Spencer Fry

While the world looks upon you as an inspiration to them, being the founder of a company is not easy. Founding a company injects a lot of responsibility. Founders often underestimate the fiduciary and moral responsibility that goes with raising and implementing capital. When you are a founder, you become the steward of money, hopes, and ambitions, yours as well as of the others.

And of course, your job is on the line too. Your investors and employees have invested their faith in you and this not only honors you but also burdens you with a bigger responsibility—that the people who believe in you, the company, and your mission, whether investors or employees, have put their faith ultimately in you. It is a tremendous honor and burden simultaneously. As I stated earlier, no startup can enjoy a steady stream of revenue in the first 1000 days and every founder needs to sacrifice their potential development in the previous career path. Moreover, during the initial days, every startup goes through a zig-zag path and faces innumerable and unexpected risks.

Startup IS NOT For The Faint-hearted

Despite the founder's experience and hard work, there are a few factors that are considered startup killers and emphasize the fact that a startup is not for the faint-hearted.

- Are you prepared for unforeseen expenses? You might have calculated the cost of the raw materials, cost of equipment, office space rent, and labor costs and left no stone unturned. Even your profit margin is set; but what if the equipment is flawed or the raw materials incur more expenses? There exist unforeseen expenses that can chomp your profit margins, and your startup dreams can shrink overnight.
- Is your process consistent? Although a startup needs improvising at every step during the initial period, try to inculcate consistency right from the beginning. Too much alternation is never good if you are trying to make a profit.
- Frauds often come with a white-collar. There are many high-level business clients who would stiff you on the bill: they consume your services, energy, and time, and refuse to pay in the end.

- ➢ Are you lacking motivation halfway through? Startups demand a lot of hard work, long hours, and weekend work while major setbacks and financial stress are common. Losing motivation halfway is dreadful and if you are not passionate enough to build your empire, business is not for you.
- ➢ Hiring and firing can be gut-wrenching. As a founder, you need to build a strong team having appropriate talents. Good talents come with a good price. Your competitors are always trying to snatch your best employees.
- ➢ Have you planned ahead of them? Are you constantly improvising your product? Entrepreneurship does not stop with launching a new product in the market. Remember, the market is volatile and every alternate day another great mind is trying to conceive a better idea. A startup is a 24/7 involvement of constantly seeking out newer avenues to encroach.

Let us have a quick fact check on the Indian startup scenario. As per a report published on www.livemint.com, an IBM institute conducted a study on startup failures in India. Although Startup India has claimed to be a runaway success, the study claims that 90 percent of Indian startups fail within the first five years of inception. According to the program, over 27,000 startups were registered till 2020, with over 150,000 jobs created. For a country with over 12 million graduates entering the job market annually, it does not sound like much of a success. Startup India would complete six years in 2022; however, it is too early to call India an 'innovation nation.'

Startup: Playing With Risk 24/7

As the people geared up for binge-watching in the year 2020, Scam 1992 was one of the web series that made a permanent impression by showcasing the life of Harshad Mehta.

A dialogue that ran riot in the market was *"Risk hain tou ishq hai."* A startup is a roller coaster ride of playing around with a multitude of risks. Entrepreneurs are risk-takers by nature, or at minimum calculated visionaries with a clear plan of action to launch a new product or service to fill a gap in the industry. On a personal level, many entrepreneurs take big risks by leaving their stable jobs to throw their efforts and money into building a name for themselves.

There is no guaranteed monthly income and no guarantee of success, and spending time with family and friends can be a challenge in the early days of launching a company. Some of the most common risks that every entrepreneur and investor should evaluate and minimize before starting a business are as follows:

Financial Risk	Strategic Risk	Technology Risk
Entrepreneurs should have a financial plan within the overall business plan showing income projections, how much cash will be required to break even, and the expected return for investors in the first five-year timeframe. Failure to accurately plan leads to bankruptcy.	An impressive business plan will appeal to investors. However, we live in a dynamic and fast-paced world where strategies can become outdated quickly as soon as the demands take a new turn.	Humanity is thriving at the Fourth Industrial Revolution where every alternate day is introducing a paradigm shift with disruptive technologies. Entrepreneurs must brace themselves for this.

Competitive Risk	Reputational Risk
If there are no competitors at all, it is highly possible that	If a new company disappoints consumers in the initial stages,

| there is no demand for the product. If there are a few larger competitors, the market might be saturated and your company might struggle to snatch their loyal customers. | it may never gain traction. Social media plays a huge role in business reputation and word-of-mouth marketing. One tweet or negative post from an angered customer can lead to huge losses in revenue. |

Political, Environmental, and Economic Risk
Leaving aside the natural disasters like earthquakes, tornadoes, and hurricanes, or a pandemic like COVID, there may be political or man-made causes that can ruin your business too, such as wars and recessions. Countries with unstable political conditions or unstable and unsafe logistics, tax rates, or tariffs might make trade difficult.

Consider a feasibility study before plunging into the startup world. A feasibility study would help you analyze the economic, technical, legal, and scheduling considerations, to learn the probability of completing the project successfully.

Why Do Startups Fail?

Any business venture starts with the aim of achieving success; however, most successful entrepreneurs experience some failures along the way. Setbacks are discouraging; nevertheless, they do provide lessons and experiences that can lead to eventual success. Whether your business is a retail store, restaurant, hair salon, consulting company, or tech startup, you are prone to failure in the first couple of years. According to Bloomberg, only 20 percent of new businesses find success within their first 18 months. Data from entrepreneur.com and the Small Business Administration suggest that only 30 percent of new ventures succeed to the ten-year mark.

More often, entrepreneurs recognize failure as a part of success. Lack of goal attainment, low levels of revenue and profit, losing out on clients and investors describe a failed business. Loss of assets like revenue, equipment, and capital do cause trauma for the business owner. However, these failures often help entrepreneurs improve the outcomes for their next business. Failures provide lessons to curate success.

"No matter what one does, regardless of failure or success, the experience is a form of success in itself." – Jack Ma

There are some common contributors to the failure of a business, which can be broadly divided into four categories: Marketing, Management, Financial, and Innovation. However, legal challenges, too, contribute to failure.

Top 20 Reasons Startups Fail
Based on an Analysis of 101 Startups Post-Mortems

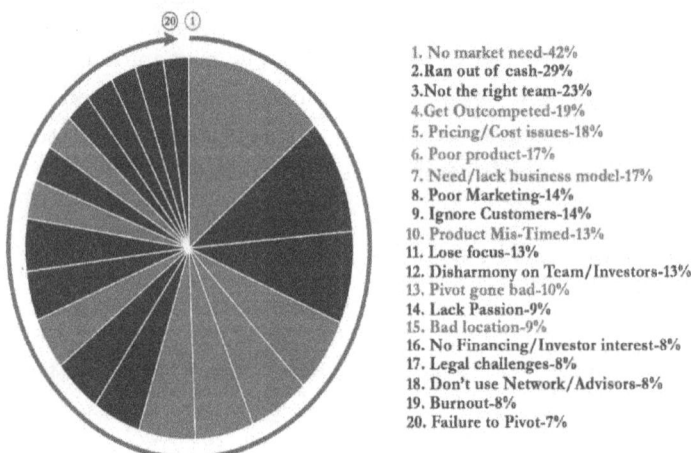

1. No market need-42%
2. Ran out of cash-29%
3. Not the right team-23%
4. Get Outcompeted-19%
5. Pricing/Cost issues-18%
6. Poor product-17%
7. Need/lack business model-17%
8. Poor Marketing-14%
9. Ignore Customers-14%
10. Product Mis-Timed-13%
11. Lose focus-13%
12. Disharmony on Team/Investors-13%
13. Pivot gone bad-10%
14. Lack Passion-9%
15. Bad location-9%
16. No Financing/Investor interest-8%
17. Legal challenges-8%
18. Don't use Network/Advisors-8%
19. Burnout-8%
20. Failure to Pivot-7%

Marketing Failure: Having the 'me-too' mentality in the absence of a unique selling proposition can be damaging for any startup. A clearly defined competitive advantage is the key factor to hold your business in the market. The next essential component of marketing failure is missing out on the potential customer.

A startup market communication should focus on the target audience. You cannot sell a kid's toy to an adult who needs an app to control mail spam. Improper positioning of your product in the market will definitely lead you to failure.

Management Failure: One of the major contributors to startup failure is the loss of excitement in the business. For example, Joel Delgado had launched El Paso Disaster Room 915 in 2015 and had developed this business along with his three friends right after college. The business was very well received by the younger generation as a new mode of entertainment. However, within 3 years Delgado lost his interest and switched his career to teaching. Similarly, cofounder conflict is common and often leads to management failure. How can we forget about Steve Jobs being asked to leave his own company in 1985? Lack of planning with respect to succession, marketing strategy, and equity division can cause conflict amongst the top management, which if not handled strategically can lead to business dissolution.

Financial Failure: Lack of cash flow, dearth of working capital, and too much debt are common sharks that can dissolve any startup. Loans can provide some assistance while working to build the clientele; however, if the business does not grow and develop a sustainable cash flow, its ability to operate will come to an end.

Innovation Failure: Startups that do not change their strategies, technology, or products run the risk of endangering the business. Similarly, change should come with the right adjustment. Every startup must carry a build-measure-learn loop to avoid these pitfalls by recognizing what consumers really want and need by doing a strategic market study.

Legal challenges: Legal regulations and complexities often strangulate startups. Government reforms like demonetization lead to a sudden fund crunch in the market.

It affects the finances of startups. Zebpay and Koinex could not survive the legal challenges faced after the RBI directive banning cryptocurrency transactions.

Fear of Losing: Even a constant fear of failure can make your business fail. Fear freezes entrepreneurs and forces them into a corner instead of advancing their businesses. Fear prevents them from reaching potential clients and being profitable. When a startup struggles to make ends meet, the owners experience many emotions, like pain, grief, shame, humiliation, self-blame, anger, and hopelessness. Business failure is always taken as a personal failure, as the startup has been the identity of the entrepreneur. Managing these emotions can help business owners heal and continue moving forward to their next business. Reaching out for help to a trusted mentor or therapist can provide guidance in dealing with these feelings.

And as Elon Musk quoted, *"Failure is an option here. If things are not failing, you are not innovating enough."* James Dyson, founder and inventor of the Dyson vacuum cleaner, had failed 5,126 times before he came up with his Dual Cyclone vacuum cleaner in 1993. It was fifteen years after he had created the first version. In his own words, *"Failure is interesting—it's part of making progress. You never learn from success, but you do learn from failure. When I created the Dual Cyclone vacuum, I started out with a simple idea, and by the end, it got more audacious and interesting. I got to a place I never could have imagined because I learned what worked and didn't work."*

The importance of failing lies in learning how to get back up again. Eric Ries dove into failure with his first company and it was painful to let go of an unsuccessful idea. He then applied his lessons to create his new virtual reality company IMVU, which became a very successful experiment and he derived the lean startup method. Failure often pinpoints the shortcomings and lets an entrepreneur find ways to better their performance. Let us have a look at some of the failed startups in India and the reason behind their pronounced failure.

Startup Company	Founding Year	Sector	Reason For Failure
Pepper Tap	2014	Grocery	Cash Burn and zero inventory owned
Doodhwala	2015	Hyperlocal, Grocery	Decreased download, controversy
Local Banya	2014	eCommerce	Intense competition, lapses in business model
Yumist	2017	Food delivery	High operational cost
iProf	2009	EdTech	Low adoption
Purple Squirrel	2013	EdTech	Dipping Sales
Loan Meet	2015	Fintech	Failed to raise funds
Zebpay	2014	Crypto	Legal challenges
Cardback	2012	Fintech	Wrong timing, improper market research
Doc Talk	2016	HealthTech	Inability to Pivot
Baby Berry	2014	Child health tech	Improper revenue model
Jabong	2012	Virtual Mall	Financial mismanagement
Shopo	2017	Handicraft ecommerce	Poor service quality
Hike	2012	Social network	Complexities
Parcelled	2014	Logistic	Poor pricing mechanism
Freshconnect	2018	Agritech	Bad

			management
Dial-a-celeb	2018	Entertainment	Failed business model
Roder	2014	Transportation	High operational cost
Intelligent Interface	2015	Software solution	Legal technicalities
InoWorx	2010	IT solutions	Poor management
Rooms Tonite	2014	Hospitality	Cash crunch and intense competition
JoBridge	2017	Job consultancy	Failed business model

Most of these entrepreneurs started new businesses with the idea of driving the economy, innovation, and job creation. However, about half of those new businesses fail in the first five years, and two out of three last less than a decade. A close look at their failure stories can easily summarize the common factors that Indian entrepreneurs have been overlooking.

- Most of the entrepreneurs were not prepared with the capital it would take to operate the business. Whether they bootstrap or take the Shark Tank approach, they miscalculated a lot.
- Misreading the market and the customers' demands while facing intense competition with the established players.
- Businesses were not well-thought-out with long-term and short-term goals. Many of them failed because they did not have clear success benchmarks along the way. Many entrepreneurs forget that Amazon or TATA was not built in a day. Having unrealistic targets to join the Fortune 500 lists can lead to nothing but failure.

- Trying to be everything to every customer is as futile as an elephant thinking it can fly. Failure of Hike is one of the best examples in this category. Lazy marketing killed many good products and services.
- A startup is not a sluggish affair. An entrepreneur must be a smart worker while constantly checking on the loopholes created by the competitors.
- Poor management and planning killed Inoworx and Baby Berry, to name a couple. They neither constructed a well-planned business model nor did they watch the competition. Failing to accept constructive criticism moved a few of those aforementioned startups closer to failure.
- Soft skills like working attitude, communication, empathy, networking, and leadership skills are essential for success. Improper delegation is a curse.
- Starting a business is a 24/7 job in most cases, and if you do not delegate tasks to the right talent, your long-term goals are going for a toss.

"Entrepreneurs are the only people who will work 80 hours a week to avoid working 40 hours a week."
–Lori Greiner

How To Cope With Failure?

The first step in failure is the impending 'fear of failure.' If as an entrepreneur you are anticipating failure, you must modify your business strategy by changing the target outcomes for your business. Instead of aiming to make millions in the first six months, make your beginning with a leaner start, learning about your customers and how best to serve them. Most of the time, learning and growth goals are as valuable as hitting a revenue target to conceive an overall success and longevity. On the same note, an unmet goal is not equivalent to complete failure.

Refocus on the experience gained and revise your goal. A startup is stressful and often creates health issues because of its unending grind. Never ignore the proverbial way of living–health is indeed wealth. Meditation or breathing exercises help in lowering the anxiety created by fearful thinking. Reaching out to a mentor, support group, therapist, or counselor can also help alleviate the emotional turmoil. Try to convert the lessons of failure into success by following these tips.

- One failure is not the end of all.
- Experiment with your business and try new things. Business is not for the faint-hearted, and so never be a risk-averter.
- Listen to your gut. Failure often implants the power of intuition.
- Seek feedback. Repeatedly and unashamedly.
- Be flexible toward change.
- Keep the learning door open.

"Do not be embarrassed by your failures. Learn from them and start again."
–Richard Branson

Failing Is Not Equal To Losing

There are several factors that often function as multipliers in the world of startups: wrong product, a misfit in the market, intense competition, depletion of capital, bad partnership, regulatory hurdles, or bad hiring, and the list continues. Any hiccup in the system has the power to threaten the whole existence of the business. Failure is probably a default state of startups and 90 percent of the startups fail, with 75 percent being venture-backed startups. It is indeed every entrepreneur's desire to avoid failures, but as failure is inevitable, it is equally meaningful to embrace one's failure and learn lessons to avoid further replication and implications. In this section, let us discuss what successful entrepreneurs learned from their failures.

Negative feedbacks are useful, so says Carrie Chan, Cofounder and CEO of Avant Meats. When two of their investors pointed out the loopholes, they could shape their future strategies regarding their product idea. Similarly, the company had received negative feedback about their suboptimal marketing strategy, and soon they shifted their focus.

While Kasim Alfalahi of Avanci points out the pivotal role of company culture and organizational goal, he links his success to his ability to act quickly as and when his employees were distracted from the organizational goal. In the Indian market, embracing the change has been a regular affair.

Biocon's Kiran Mazumdar Shaw became a household name for women entrepreneurs as she encroached in the domain of brewing science. Sea6 Energy was founded in 2010 while providing a solution to India's overconsumption of energy and thus started a new path of startups in the energy sector.

Sunil Bharti Mittal started his first business and made crankshafts for bicycles when he was only 18 years old. He did not see much profit in the initial days, but by 1980, he had established the Bharti Overseas Trading Company, through which he imported portable electric power generators. And then, in 1983, the government banned the import of generators. Mr. Mittal went out of business overnight. But that did not stop him as he found success through the telecom business and started marketing fax machines and telephones, which helped him become successful.

There are several inspiring stories of startups failing and then rising back to become a unicorn. The bottom line is to learn from your mistakes and accept and reflect on your failures. Refocus on your passion and keep pursuing your aim, no matter what. Failure is not about losing and you can understand this better if you separate your identity from your business. There are many entrepreneurs out there who do not succeed at the first attempt. Every stalwart in the world of business would ask new-age entrepreneurs to be dedicated and passionate to succeed after failure.

"We failed an important demo, but our ability to stand up and to admit the price of that mistake ended up being a big win. As an organization, we learned to look for our mistakes in all the steps prior to the demo. This created a level of accountability which supported the team members who were directly interfacing with the client as the demo failed. I remember going from a sense of complete failure to "we will recover and grow stronger" in a few hours. I realized that failure means learning something, and we learned a lot that day. We also ended up winning that account and the rest is history."
–Meirav Oren, Cofounder and CEO, Versatile

Is Hiring Process Linked To Startup Success?

Several failed startups showcase the significance of having the right talent in the startup team. If an innovative idea forms the soul of a startup, the hiring process constructs the DNA. Choosing the first 10 employees needs critical thinking as they are going to be the benchmark for the next 100. A strategic and systematic approach to hiring offers the right direction to avoid failure. After funding, the biggest barrier in a startup's growth is placing the right talent for the right job at the right time. Hiring your first employees is exciting and a significant milestone for any startup. Similarly, it has its own challenges.

If you hire the right people, you will bring on board the skills and experience needed to grow your company and develop your product. However, a single wrong hire can push you back. Growing your startup beyond the founding team is daunting and challenging because a startup is often perceived as a high-risk opportunity and you are an unknown name in the employment market. When a startup grows beyond the founding team, every new addition to the team changes the startup's DNA. A good hire expresses new ways to succeed in the market and similarly, a bad hire is more like a mutant gene. A misfit employee can affect your team's culture and can cast a negative impact on the work environment, productivity levels, and overall motivation.

The success of your startup depends on your ability to build a team of great people. There are several things a founder must ensure while attracting top talent. Build a company that is worthy to work for. Sorting out your identity as an employer, nailing down your company's cultural values, and making the most of your social presence are some of the major steps in the initial process of attracting the right talent.

Define the company's value on the website. Defining and sharing your company values is a great starting point from which you can begin to evaluate prospective employees based on culture fit, which is essential for building a close-knit startup team.

Keeping a strategic approach to the company's website content and social media presence increases the startup's value in the eyes of prospective employees. While hiring the right talent is important, retention is crucial too. A competitive pay package is necessary to avoid losing good people from your team. Make recruiting a continuous process. Keep the search on even when you do not have an immediate need, as building connections is good for any startup. Building an attractive company helps convince potential employees that they want to join your startup, and will attract inbound leads who are interested in your product, team, and company culture.

"Personal relationships are far and away the biggest source of talent."
–Tom DeVoto

Are you networking enough? Attending conferences, talks, or tech meetups are great ways to grow your network. On the same note, if networking is a passive way of hiring, sourcing is the active path. Active outreach helps in bringing new talent through the existing talent. Always share the next-hire requirement with your team and beat quantity with quality. Get potential employees with previous startup experience. Candidates with prior experience working in a startup will be better equipped to cope and adapt to a fast-paced startup environment than someone who has been working in a corporate environment for years.

Have you thought of freelancers? Considering the cash crunch, if you cannot afford a full-time employee yet, you might want to consider hiring freelancers. Many freelancers are keen to join a fast-growing startup in the early days. It also gives you a chance to see how they work, and if they are a mutual fit. If the freelancer performs well, then you can approach them for a full-time role.

Building a fantastic startup team is a continuous act of prioritization. The founders need to constantly make decisions about who the next hire should be, based on the ever-changing needs of their startup's workload and the team's skill set, and when they should be looking to hire, based on the fluctuations in the workload and the types of work required.

As your startup grows, the priorities change from product development to reaching prospective customers, to acquiring paying customers, and then, to retaining them. Consecutively, the type of roles you are most commonly hiring for will change over time. For example, when the startup is focusing on product development, it needs more developers than customer support personnel. And by the time it has got a sizeable customer base, it must invest more in customer success in order to improve customer retention. Thus, the stage of a startup is linked with the hiring process.

Similarly, keeping an inventory of the existing team's skills, compared to the types of work the startup is doing is necessary. As the team's workload changes, the gaps will appear and additional team members can be brought in. Another important aspect is to know when to hire. Hiring too early can leave you hard-pressed for cash, and hiring too late can leave your team struggling under an ever-mounting workload.

Deciding when to hire is a delicate balancing act where one must weigh in the following points:

- Can you afford to bring on a new hire?
- Do you have the workload to support a new hire?
- Do you have time to recruit and onboard a new hire, before your team's workload becomes overwhelming?

"It is more difficult to find, hire and retain people whose backgrounds are not presently represented at your company... If you have 10 employees who are all men, you will find it far more difficult to find, hire and retain women. Women who interview with you will be skeptical about how inclusive your company is when there is little evidence to support it." – Adam Pisoni, Abl Schools

Is Startup Hazardous To Health?

Being your own boss 24/7 for 365 days is not child's play. While there are many perks of being the head honcho, the burden of pursuing success in entrepreneurship can be enormous if the entrepreneurs forget their well-being. Startups are never for the faint-hearted as they involve a continuous grind to be better with each passing day. Before you plunge into this fruitful career, you must acknowledge the hardships involved.

Entrepreneurial research has pointed out some of the key health hazards.

- **Depression**: Dr. Michael Freeman, a clinical professor at UCSF and an entrepreneur himself, researched only to find that 49 percent of the surveyed group of entrepreneurs undergo bouts of depression.
- **Anxiety**: In the same study, 27 percent of the entrepreneurs had anxiety issues. How can India ever forget the suicide note of CCD's VG Siddhartha?
- **Addiction**: Behavioral addiction toward gambling and social media obsession are common and often lead to guilt, high levels of strain, and abuse of foods, alcohol, or even drugs.
- **Hypertension/Heart Disease**: It is no secret that being responsible for the financial prosperity of others as well as the overall success of a business can be quite stressful. High stress has been shown to temporarily raise one's blood pressure and can trigger habits such as unhealthy eating, which can lead to heart disease.

- **Lack of Health Insurance**: It is a known fact in the business world that solopreneurs often choose covering everyday necessities over paying high monthly insurance premiums.
- **Spine problems**: Entrepreneurs have been found to work 63 percent longer than the average worker, and many spend a lot of that time at a desk, behind a computer, or on their smartphones. Many falls prey to conditions such as sciatica and spondylitis.
- **Insomnia**: With a large percentage of founders working at least 52 to 70 hours per week, there is hardly any time left for sleep. Experts recommend six to eight hours of sleep a day, but entrepreneurs who work long hours are probably only getting a maximum of four hours.
- **Eyesight issues**: Keeping the company's vision right is a path of self-sacrifice. The average adult spends 11 hours per day on gadgets, and entrepreneurs are more than attached to their smartphones, laptops, and computers. Entrepreneurs often face computer vision syndrome, also referred to as digital eye strain.
- **Migraines**: Constant stress on high performance often leads to irregular food habits and brings life to a vicious cycle of health issues.
- **Hormonal Health**: Hormone suppression is common leading to several metabolic disorders.

Come what may, a startup is a journey of patience and perseverance. Every human has to do something to survive. None can escape from moving the hand to the mouth if one wants to eat. A startup needs 24/7 involvement and it certainly is demanding. However, as Narendra Modi says, *"Hard work never brings fatigue. It brings satisfaction."*

Key Takeaways:

- Entrepreneurs need to be bold
- Learn the reasons behind a startup's failure
- Understand the rule of the hiring process
- Pros and cons of entrepreneurship are two sides of the same coin

PART 3
THE KEY TO EFFECTIVE PLANNING

8

SUCCESSION PLANNING: PREPARING BUSINESS FOR FUTURE

Check out the pages of World History: empires without proper succession planning eventually withered away. We no longer live under the reigns of kings and queens, but the principles of economic growth still revolve around concrete succession planning. Any business, be it traditional or a startup, is built with prolonged efforts and effective planning. Every businessman conceives the idea of building a business empire to leave behind a legacy. Passing the baton is neither easy nor escapable; rather it is an essential factor that comes with its own challenges. If building a business from scratch needs time, so does true succession planning. For every business, it is imperative to understand that succession planning is a thoroughly examined process and not just an event to celebrate.

> *"Succession Planning is one of the essential components of broader human resource planning. It is a systemic approach for identifying, developing and retaining productive employees to perform in projected business objectives."*
> – Chad Hill

An Overview of Succession Planning

The idea is to nurture a strong leadership pipeline for the organization. You have to understand that there is no dearth of talent as the talent pool is constantly evolving with new opportunities. You, as an employer, cannot prohibit your employees from looking for better avenues, but at the same time, you have to work smart to maintain the momentum of your own business. The first step in the ladder of succession planning is high-potential identification. There are some specific competencies required and only a few employees are actually capable of critical leadership positions. No founder would like to leave the business in the hands of a poor leader. Succession planning is not just about finding a replacement or successor for an existing business leader. An extensive employee development plan resides at the corner. The high-performers of any organization actively engage in this process of succession planning.

An effective succession plan looks for some desirable traits like intellect, aptitude, agility, and the propensity to lead. There are a few other aspects to consider. Always remember that you have put your heart and soul, 24/7 of hard work to build your business by taking several risks. Your successor should be willing to step outside the comfort zone and welcome challenges instead of fearing them. As a founder, you would have run for 10 to 15 years to build a high-performing team of like-minded people. Your successor should be a better version of you, with effective leadership skills, and someone who knows how to empower and assist others to contribute their best. Before you decide to leave your business in someone else's hands, analyze if the chosen successor is a good learner. Without consistent learning, there is no growth involved.

In this chase of identifying and developing future leaders at your company, the aim is to keep the business running and make the organization prepared for all the outcomes and possibilities in advance. The founders often circle the high-performers in advance for the potential succession.

With immense leadership qualities and brilliant communication skills, any employee, irrespective of the present position, can become a good successor. Identification is a gradual process and founders should never wait for a crisis to happen. Test-running the employees and promoting in-house talent bear better fruit than hiring someone from the outside.

One of the most essential components of any business is loyalty. In-bred talents would know the struggles of the organization and the loopholes better to give the much-needed thrust. Additionally, you have to understand that although identification and succession planning both fall under the cadre of human resourcing, the latter is a more focused approach to building a better leader.

Succession planning is like future-proofing your business in the changing market scenario. Here are some of the key points every founder shall ponder upon while making a succession plan:

- Your existing top talent may not remain with you forever; thus, strive for a talent-building pipeline.
- Hiring talent from outside may be expensive and involves high chances of conflict with the existing team.
- Providing growth and developmental opportunities to the existing talent ensures the future success of the organization and helps in higher employee engagement and retention.

It is indeed a great idea to link your inbred talent to succession planning to ensure the holistic and sustainable growth of your organization in the present and the future. It not only enables you to plan for organizational emergencies but also ensures that your talent pool is vested in the future of the organization.

"Succession planning often results in the selection of a weaker representation of yourself. Avoid This!
— Peter Drucker

Succession Planning For Startups

For a family-run business like Reliance or Mahindra & Mahindra, the succession process is quite smooth. It is much similar to the idea of inheritance. Dhirubhai Ambani was succeeded by his two sons: Mukesh Ambani and Anil Ambani. It is more like taking forward your legacy. Commoners often think that succession is for big companies; however, a planned succession is about keeping the business alive in the growing market. Succession planning is in fact very crucial for startups and smaller companies.

Entrepreneurs must recognize that in a startup, the departure of a top employee creates a huge impact. Succession planning is needed not only for the top position like a CEO or CFO but for the middle management level as well. A succession plan should be proactive, with employees diversifying their experience and getting trained for effective skills.

As an entrepreneur, do understand the long-term direction of your startup. Without an effective strategic plan guiding your ladder of growth and diversification, you cannot plan for a better successor. Analyze the lack in the present system; the one who takes over must be capable of bridging the gap. Your team must focus on the key areas that require continuity and development of your employees. Currently, the Indian startups are growing fast and many are coming into the bigger league of unicorns, which makes succession planning an inevitable strategy. Do you know that 73 percent of Indian investors are not happy with the succession planning strategies of their investee companies?

> *"The investor perspective is risk mitigation. If the investee company doesn't have a clear No. 2 or No. 3 in place and the leader quits, searches can take six-nine months to close. It is a lifetime in a high growth startup; hence, investors are stressing the need for talent pipeline and risk mitigation."*
> — Arjun Erry

Succession planning in startups may not fit easily in the minds of the cofounders. A lot of intellectuals in the market believe that succession planning for startups is premature thinking. Business continuity seems more important than succession planning. Moreover, startups usually have more than one founder, and a default succession plan is negotiated within the founding team. Beyond the founders, many startups are led by a board, and execution is left to the founders and senior management.

The investors of a startup, of course, look into the aspect of succession planning differently. The cofounders play a vital role in bringing in the investment. Investors would not be sure to remain with the startup if the founding bodies change. However, there is a wave of progressive thinking where founders are propagating the culture of succession planning to combat adverse situations. Sometimes though, passing the baton becomes difficult amid fears of wrong cultural fit.

You have to understand that a startup founder's brain is differently conceived as compared to the corporate honchos. There lies a big gap between established business houses and burgeoning startups, which often puts off seasoned corporate leaders from joining even a matured and profit-making startup. In the previous chapter, you have seen the statistics of failed startups. As the list of failed startups is competitive enough, investors are presently giving a wake-up call to boards. Succession planning is not a mere box to tick. In the present scenario, where the business world is facing unparalleled transformation, succession planning is viewed as a pivotal process to shape the future of any startup company. Having the right executives in place at the right time does not happen overnight. It happens through a rigorous selection and development process involving thoughtful planning and upfront conversation.

Steps Of Succession Planning

As stated, succession planning is a gradual process and every founder must go through some of the key steps.

- Have you identified the critical positions in your startup? As a founder, you have to do an impact assessment to find out which role is most critical and vulnerable.
- Have you profiled the key competencies? This step shall let your employees better understand the key responsibilities of the position. The competencies should highlight the qualifications as well as the behavioral and technical competencies required to perform the role successfully.
- What is your talent management strategy? You must choose the talent management strategies you wish to implement to address succession planning. These strategies may span career development, training, and recruitment.
- Have you implemented the strategies? Document your chosen strategies in an action plan and start to implement them. Make sure your action plan clearly defines timelines, roles, and responsibilities.
- Are you evaluating? To ensure that your succession planning efforts succeed, regularly monitor the effectiveness of the plan. Evaluate its related activities and make the necessary amendments.

When To Have Succession Plan?

Business professionals deal with a miasma of risks and challenges and the process of transferring the ownership, management, and interest of a business is sometimes heart-wrenching. Now, what is the ideal time to make a succession plan? A succession plan is required through the survival, growth, and maturity stages of a business. All business owners, partners, and shareholders should have a plan in place during these business stages. While you pave the path for your successor, you must be aware of your financial objectives for yourself, your family, and the business.

You cannot plan for succession, leave everything behind, and come to the road. If you have chosen business as a profession, every aspect of it must benefit you and your family. Business succession planning involves legal, tax, and personal financial issues. Guidance from a qualified attorney or tax professional is strongly recommended.

There are two approaches toward succession in the case of multiple business owners.

- **Entity Plan:** In this arrangement, each of the business owners has a separate agreement with the corporation or partnership as the entity. The entity, as per the buy-sell agreement, will buy the other partners' interests once they decide to leave.
- **Cross Purchase Agreement:** In this situation, a cross purchase agreement is established between each of the owners. When one of the owners leaves, the surviving owners agree to buy a proportionate share of the departing owner's interest.

Buy-Sell arrangements are a simple, yet effective way for business owners of privately held companies to plan for the orderly transfer of business interests where two or more owners are actively involved in the business. In addition to securing the needs of the surviving family members and ensuring the continuation of the business, a buy-sell arrangement also ensures each owner that there is a buyer for their business interest at a fair price.

The ideal time to start succession planning is when your business is starting to take off. It is possible to safeguard your business without it being an overwhelming process. The best thing you can do for your company is to start the succession planning process now. Do not put your business, the financial lives of your employees, or your personal financial situation at risk. Instead, take the time well in advance to plan out a thoughtful business ownership succession plan.

By starting early, you also reduce the amount of work you and your stakeholders will have to take on later in the game. If you start as soon as a person is hired, you are also forced to do workforce planning, which is a way to make sure that your talent aligns with your goals.

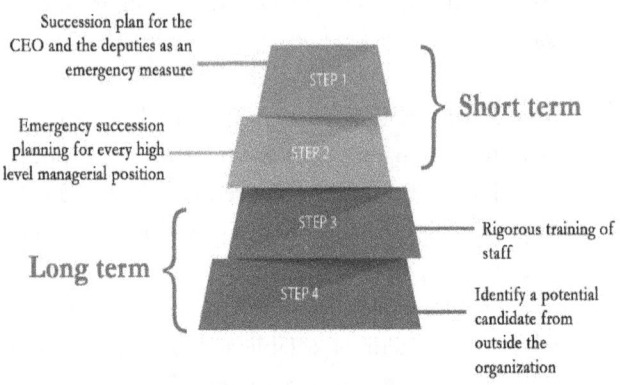

Perils Of Not Having A Succession Plan Ready

In the case of business continuity, preparation is the best policy. The absence of a clear succession plan can pose a serious risk to businesses. We all are thriving in an extremely fast-paced world and it becomes difficult to find the time to plan for succession. It is imperative to not get caught up in the day-to-day administration of the job and presume that the high-performing employees shall never leave.

Let me tell you, any high-performer is constantly looking for diversified experience and the statistics prove that rarely does a person spend more than three years in a single company. The first employer of the high-performers teaches them the tricks of the trade. The second job provides them with the experience, and soon they switch to start their own company or they opt for diversification of their skills. -

A company's succession plan helps to retain these high performers and often helps to maintain the company's image in the market. Let us look at the case scenario of a common man buying shares of a particular company because it is run by someone well-known in the market. The moment that well-known man steps out, the share prices would take a plunge and the common man is likely to lose an ounce of belief in the company. What if the well-known man leaves the company without naming a successor behind him?

Failing to name/leave a successor in place is akin to opening the proverbial Pandora's Box! The ensuing risks and problems would be numerous.

- **Financial risk:** Sudden vacancy in a company's leadership injects the fear of uncertainty, which is enough to cause financial damage. Whether you are a startup or an established business, investors scare easily and may end up withdrawing their support.
- **Knowledge void:** When a top employee leaves the company, they take their wealth of knowledge with them. There prevails a void of knowledge about the systems, processes, and customers. Any company runs well with the transition of knowledge. Without succession planning, the knowledge remains cocooned within one person and does not benefit the company in the long run.
- **Instigate internal power struggles:** Without a clear succession plan, employees may compete for the position and engage in power struggles to take the vacant spot. Internal conflict causes a volatile work environment that demotivates every employee.
- **Resentment in the supply chain:** The leader is always the face of the company. Every vendor or client or customer looks at the leader before opting for the product. A great leader makes a customer believe in the company's product and helps to bring in investors, new clients, and vendors.

If the response time slips or customer service dips many customers may decide to take their business elsewhere.

- **Rise in attrition rate:** Business leaders form the root of the organizational culture. A good leader leaving often demotivates the employees as they fail to find the path to follow in their career growth.
- **Hiring or promoting mistakes:** In some cases, when the position of a CEO or any other leadership position suddenly becomes vacant, the need to quickly fill that position leads to choosing the wrong candidate for the role. Whether they are hired from outside the company or promoted from within, hiring someone who is not fully qualified to handle the position is a costly mistake. This urgency to hire someone can result in an inflated salary and benefits package in order to quickly fill the role.
- **Actual talent is overlooked:** Without a clear succession plan, it can be easy to overlook candidates internally who may be interested in a leadership role. These candidates are often a great investment as they are already in the company and understand the business. In most cases, it is also cheaper to promote within the company than it is to hire outside of it, especially in the case of executive and leadership roles. Hiring talent from within can strengthen their commitment to the company and protect the company from losing any skills or business knowledge, which would happen if these employees left.

It is crucial to understand that succession planning is about more than filling gaps or finding replacement candidates. The goal of succession planning is to ensure a smooth transition. While preparing for growth, development, and transition, you must lay the foundation for an effective succession plan by aligning the concept with the vision and mission of the business. Building a scalable and dependable leadership in the pipeline is indeed difficult;

Nevertheless, companies that invest in succession planning are clued-up for competitive advantage, and are more prepared for turbulence in a rapidly changing economy.

Succession In Family Businesses

Business runs in the veins: how many times have you heard this? In India, 85 percent of the businesses are family owned. Transferring the reins to the next generation is like inheriting a permanent source of income. However, times have changed. A farmer's son sees the hardships of his father and tries to look out for greener pastures to earn more for himself and his family. A doctor's daughter realizes the 24/7 work schedule of her parents and starts detesting the whole medical profession. Similar situations do crop up in business families too. As stated at the very beginning of the book, we all have cultural and social factors that influence us while planning for our future. Not every Gujarati businessman's son wishes to follow the steps of his father. There are many who crossed the realms of the family business and switched to an entirely different profession. Inducting the next generation into the family business is not an easy task, that too when the world is flourishing with so many different opportunities.

India's family-run businesses are successful in making significant contributions to the growth of the Indian economy. However, the transition face is often challenging and historically there has been a low success rate in managing transitions across generations. Succession planning is vital for preserving a family business. Nurturing and developing the next generation to take over the reins is the most daunting issue faced by the owners of family businesses. Can you believe that only one-third of the Indian family businesses transfer the ownership but not the management to the next generation? Many family-run businesses have brought in professionals for managing the business. Introducing professionals seems to be a better option when the next generation is not capable or confident to take up leadership positions.

Apart from this, succession in family businesses has its own unique challenges like overlapping roles of family members, differing views of the current and the next generation, or a sheer lack of family governance structure. There looms an emotional challenge in family dynamics. Choosing a successor from the family may compromise personal relationships or create irreconcilable family rifts. The case worsens if all family members are active in the business. Dhirubhai Ambani's sudden demise without leaving a proper plan for Mukesh and Anil Ambani had caused enough headlines talking about sibling rifts. Moreover, in the past few decades, the generation gap has been widening at a faster pace. The current generation has an entirely different perspective, expectation, and risk-taking capability.

Apart from the bigger players in the market, there is a huge number of SMEs in the industrial areas of Vadodara, Nashik, and Pune. Most of them are manufacturing units (mainly fabrication) and have been set up by first-generation entrepreneurs. If you dig deep into their background, they are mainly engineers, and in their three decades of entrepreneurship and business life, they have made handsome profits. They tend to invest their hard-earned money into their children's better education and often send the next generation to the USA, Canada, and Australia. Unfortunately, in many cases, it has been found that the next generation remained unwilling to come back. In this scenario, the industry that has been cultivated by an entrepreneur does not see succession planning. Invariably, a business closes if the owner does not find a suitable successor.

Identifying the second line of succession, or getting young entrepreneurs to take over or come on board seems a better plan. Initially, the owner may gradually download the equity and give a chance to the young entrepreneurs to take over fully. The original owner would get a royalty for a few years. Industries Association must come forward when there is a dearth of proper succession and help make a fruitful transition. Improper succession planning leads to premature shut down of businesses: both of big companies and SMEs.

As Anil Raj Gupta, the Chairman and Managing Director of Havells India, once quoted, *"My father was a visionary. When you grow up in a self-made, first generation entrepreneur family, there will always be inter-generational gaps. If these are not managed properly, it can create rifts, which are not good for both the business and the family. We have seen dynasties crumble due to family feuds."*

Nevertheless, there are cases where the younger generation has either added new features to the way of doing business or has started their independent business. For example, 23-year-old Karan Mehta has taken his family business of Ashok Oil and Food Products to a new D2C business model apart from their usual export business. Similarly, Kavin Bharti Mittal, son of Sunil Bharti Mittal, decided not to join his family business and ventured out to set up Hike Messenger. Similarly, Kumar Mangalam Birla's children, Ananya and Aryaman, are pursuing their interest in micro-finance and cricket. Honestly, there is a kind of freedom and recognition provided to the younger generation in whichever field they choose to work in. This, in most cases, has worked wonders.

Recently, many family-run businesses have decided to separate ownership and management, which has helped to prevent a clash between the aspirations of the family members and the long-term goals of the business. In India, the trend is emerging where family businesses are creating a governance structure that clarifies norms relating to the family's involvement in the business.

Is It Time To Involve External Professionals?

The core objective in mentoring an internal candidate for succession is to ensure that the internal affairs, strategy, challenges, existing culture, and relationships within and outside the organization remain balanced. Internal talent can quickly transform into the elevated role. However, there are certain scenarios where a company must look beyond its boundary. Even the most successful organizations compare their leadership candidates with those of their peers in other companies.

Certain situations that demand an external successor are as follows:

- Though the internal candidate has the potential to lead, he/she may not be ready yet to lead the organization. In such cases, the company decides over a seasoned CEO to serve for a set period of time and mentor the internal candidate for the future.
- Small or mid-sized organizations often lack the resources to groom internal candidates for a bigger role.
- An external candidate is needed at the top when there is a need for a change in strategy and direction.

Case Study: Marico Limited – Professionalizing the Board

One of the fast-moving FMCG and skincare businesses, Marico was founded in 1990 by Harsh Mariwala. He transformed his family's traditional trading business into a leading consumer products business. In 2014, Saugata Gupta was inducted as a professional MD and Harsh Mariwala took the back seat in a non-executive role. He no longer took care of the day-to-day affairs; rather a team of professionals was inducted to run the business. Harsh Mariwala, though, remains the chairman. Why? Because Harsh Mariwala's son, Rishabh chose to diversify with his own venture. His daughter is a canine behaviorist and none of his heirs are on the Marico board. Marico Limited is a great example of introducing professionals in the business at the right time to keep the business aligned with the company's goal.

Case Study: Infosys – Conflicting Ideologies

It was indeed a game of musical chairs in the case of Infosys's succession planning. The core promoters handed over the company to a professional board; however, circumstances took a new turn and Narayana Murthy had to come back to steer the ship for a short while.

The new board had the industry veterans and they selected Vishal Sikka to lead. The IT industry was going through difficult times and his performance during his tenure was fair enough to consider him. Still, much like the Ratan Tata–Cyrus Mistry fiasco, the style of functioning and leadership became a thorn. The core promoters could not handle his style of functioning and implicitly questioned the decision-making ability of the board. Eventually, Sikka quit along with three more board members.

The problem, in this case, was that Murthy had an ideology crash. Sikka was questioned about his leadership style and it was like every core promoter was hell-bent to throw a dart at Sikka. It seemed like the founders probably forgot that even in the olden times the kings had to step down and offer the throne to the heir.

There are a few points to remember while introducing professionalism into the business.

- Mentor and groom the successor before the retiring leader moves out. For example, Deep Kalra, founder of MakeMyTrip, stepped down on February 11, 2020, and right now is holding the role of mentor.
- Grooming is progressive. For example, grooming Roshni Nadar Malhotra was always in the cards for HCL's Shiv Nadar.
- Teach the culture and norms. Your successor can be able enough but if his philosophy is different from that of your loyal employees and the organization, he/she is not a good fit.
- Giving up complete control should be done in a phased manner, and can be linked to performance.
- One can give up the management but not the entire stake or ownership. For example, Marico limited is still owned by Harsh Mariwala.
- Look for soft skills. For example, Cyrus Mistry was far-flung from the unpretentiousness of Ratan Tata.
- Do not be a fault finder, that too from the backseat.

Every founder must realize that their own role will someday require backfilling. The members of your workforce are not fixed assets and changes in human resource is inevitable. As a founder, you may not always be able to predict a valued employee's departure from the firm. But through effective succession planning, you can pave the way for the continuity so critical to your business's future.

How Does Succession Planning Fail?

Whether it is a huge business empire like TATA or a small startup like ZOHO, each position in the company matters. An abrupt absence or even a planned retirement can cripple the business if the succession planning fails to work out on time.

- **What if the successor leaves?** Despite all the best efforts to identify successors, new opportunities or personal decisions cause the next-in-line to leave the organization. Once a successor is identified, focus on leadership development and retention. In today's market where high-potential leaders are in short supply, the prospect of moving up another rung on the ladder may not be enough incentive to keep the successor on your ladder.
- **What if the incumbent does not leave?** The baby boomers often disagree to leave. Some need to keep working to fund their decimated retirement plans. Others just do not want to stop working. And a few are paid to stay to help navigate the company through uncharted waters. Very often the experienced managers and employees who stay past their expected departure date disrupt the succession plan.
- **What if the successor fails to perform?** Ill-timed placement, improper training, and a changed market are a few causes that hinder the performance of a successor.

- **Focusing on past experience is not good (always).** Too often management looks in the rearview mirror to understand what the company needs for the road ahead. An open position should be offered to someone capable of performing the new job well, not as a reward for success in the old one or 20 years of loyal service. Realize that performance and future potential are distinct and independent variables. Past performance is a good indicator but what if the emerging market demands a new skill.
- **Fixed mindset is crippling.** The heir-apparent and high-potentials are protected and pampered to avoid injuring their pride and self-esteem. They are not allowed to fail in fear of losing them to the competition. When promoted or hired into a new role, the successor with the fixed mindset works hard to protect his stature. When confronted with setbacks, challenges, or ambiguity, the pampered heir blames others. Trash the resume and focus on the successor's ability to deal with complexity, ambiguity, and volatility. Passion, the ambition to stretch, the willingness to learn, and resiliency are the hallmarks of future peak performance.
- **DO NOT complicate succession planning.** Organizational politics, bureaucracy, and time, often pile up at the back and complicate the whole process.

Lastly, before companies and business houses break their heads on succession planning, they must understand their job thoroughly. The market is always volatile and there prevails a technology intervention every now and then. A business in today's world cannot be run by a technophobic person or someone with an inflexible mindset. Critical succession planning is connected throughout the talent management process. It starts right from recruiting and moving all the way to how employee performance is managed. Before you try to hire a superstar employee, make sure your job description is correct.

And on the same note, the existing leaders must be aware of the significance of succession planning and must not cling to their authority.

> *"Clinging to the past is the problem. Embracing change is the answer."*
> – Gloria Steinem

Should You Involve Employees In Succession Planning Process?

Succession planning has the potential to benefit multiple stakeholders within an organization. The company is prepared for the future and the board fosters confidence in the leadership of your organization. And most importantly, the company's CEO feels prepared knowing that their position is covered in case of emergency. While a company prepares its succession planning, it must not overlook its largest stakeholder group, the employees. Succession aims to develop employees for future opportunities while focusing on their training needs. Additionally, a good succession plan provides transparency, which helps employees understand the path toward promotion and greater responsibility.

It gives individuals a benchmark for self-improvement and acts as a tool to guide developmental conversations between employees and leaders. Employees are certainly benefitted by the succession planning process; however, succession planning is a significant change, and not every employee harbors the courage and confidence to accept the change. A sudden change without enough context sometimes can cause concerns to many employees, leading to hesitation or mistrust of the process.

There are several benefits of involving employees in the succession planning process.

> - **Source of Motivation:** To have good candidates for a position, you need enthusiastic, talented individuals to groom for promotion.

Involving employees in the process proves that the higher management trusts them and employees are motivated to perform well. Having a motivated pool will make it easier to create benches and assign development opportunities. Employees who are engaged are always more committed, satisfied with their job, and productive in their work. These individuals are more likely to sustain their motivation over time, continuing to develop and improve their skills.

- **Faith in the Process:** If your company has never before prioritized succession planning, introducing a new process can bring about change. You need your employees to be involved in your succession plan to make them a part of the change. A participatory style of management is always encouraging and instills faith amongst the employees. Increased communication with their leaders, regular feedback sessions, and different roles and responsibilities more often stretch their skills.

- **Employees Find the Loopholes:** In the process of learning, relearning, and unlearning, employees get first-hand experience with failures. They are the true breeders of need and can identify the loopholes in the process. Robust succession plans involve understanding who is likely to retire, quit, or transfer departments. Involving employees helps the management to learn about employees' personal goals. If your employees are not invested in the process, they might not be willing to provide honest feedback on their abilities, plans, and intentions to remain, which shall further reduce the effectiveness of your succession plan.

Are You Grooming Your Successor Well?

You have been loyal to your company for a decade or more, have built up crucial relationships with vendors and suppliers, investors, and employees. You are the baby boomer of your company, and having built it from scratch, you are now willing to move ahead.

But the company needs a firm grip and demands a dependable successor. Who should replace you? Your legal heir? What if they are not prepared enough to lead your company?

For a company like the Godrej Group, Adi Godrej transformed his role from manager to mentor at the age of 73, only to give the next generation a first-hand experience at handling bigger responsibilities. Adi Godrej was adamant that if family members were not up to the task of handling the business capably as professionals, they should remain shareholders. Three years since that decision, the move has paid off and all the three Godrej scions have earned their professional stripes. They are now in charge of their respective roles, working with professionals while handling different sectors of the parent company.

The leader must understand that each employee needs to be managed and prepped for leadership differently. Leaders must customize their approach depending on the candidate's character, skills, and aptitude for learning. Make a blend of the following practices to help turn subordinates into successors:

- **Document Your Practices:** It is wonderful to verbally share the practices and processes that are central to your success, but it is even better when the information is safeguarded somewhere other than your memory. Note the effective practices in writing, codify processes, and keep a record of the best practices.
- **Demonstrate Your Proficiency:** A true leader shows the path and lets the tribe reap the benefits. No employee can follow your dictation if you do not represent your words. When candidates for succession shadow you for a day or longer, they gain a better understanding of your role and responsibilities. Demonstrate your traits and encourage job shadowing in the field.
- **Education is Crucial:** You can be born in the family of Godrej; however, that does not make you a leader by birth.

The Godrej Group's succession story is an inspiration for every business house. A successor must be taught the nitty-gritty of the business before the reins are handed over.

- **Cross-training is Essential:** The market demands diverse knowledge and a variety of skills. Training individuals on tangent job functions is beneficial to the management. When an individual learns what a colleague or manager does and how he/she does it, it raises awareness and respect, increases one's skills, and makes the individual ready for a management position. Cross-training gives flexibility.
- **Mentoring:** It is an excellent way to help employees begin to think like leaders. Two professionals, one more seasoned and the other relatively inexperienced meet regularly to learn from each other. Mentors will take an introspective look at their own processes, fine-tune their interpersonal skills, and transfer knowledge. Mentees learn best practices, expand their professional network, and learn about the pitfalls. Mentors expand a professional's understanding of the skills needed to advance in the organization, help to increase the effectiveness on the job, lend a fresh perspective, offer guidance, and address questions and problems.
- **Exposure:** As the leaders strive to pass on the knowledge, it is important that the leader also stresses the importance of retaining positive working relationships and helps successors gain visibility with high-level executives. Expose the successor to the role. Start small: maybe for a couple of days in the leader's absence. Remember, succession planning does work on the principle of 'Mic-Testing.' No successor can be put to work without testing.

As a departing leader, you should give your successors some incremental opportunities to lead while you serve as the safety net. Gradually, the comfort will increase, along with their leadership capabilities, and when the time comes for you to retire, you can trust that your legacy is left in able hands.

Any business that nurtures the dream of long-term sustenance must remain thoughtful and strategic and must set its succession plans with intention. Gathering candidates with the right amount of experience and building their resumes with timely training and diversification are the keys to growth. Succession planning can help maintain growth and stability as well as encourage retention and promotion from within.

Key Takeaways:

- Succession planning is essential to safeguard a business for the future
- Learn the steps of succession planning
- Pros and cons involved and how to manage them
- Identify the right time to include professionals in your business

Call To Action

Succession Planning is essential to prepare your business for the future. Invest time in chalking out a well-defined succession plan for your business. It is good to be principled and yet flexible in approac

9

THE BUSINESS OF GENERATING EMPLOYMENT

Do you know that by the year 2030 knocks at our door, we have to create around 90 million new jobs in the non-farm category to provide for the ~60 million people entering the workforce?

The current demographic trends forecast that an additional 30 million workers would migrate from farm-related work to the more productive non-farm-related sectors. Generating employment has become the key priority for almost all nations, especially after the pandemic. India on the other hand is sprinting fast in the scope of its growing economy. There has been a drive to increase the investments in job creation more than in any other initiative. The main goal for the next few years is going to be growth and job creation.

Have you heard of Hesa? It is a rural tech startup that works in the B2B marketplace and connects buyers and sellers from rural villages in India. Customers can buy or sell various products and perform banking and other financial activities from their villages.

Hesa services 600,000 rural customers and employs 8000+ people in over 5000 villages. Similarly, Frontier Markets is an assisted rural e-commerce platform that strives to provide quality products in 2000+ villages through a network of ~10,000+ Sahelis (rural women entrepreneurs). Sahelis invariably have a stronger grip over the customers and can curate demand for products including home appliances, mobile phones, Agri products, FMCG, cattle feed, etc. In this pursuit, Sahelis receive 10 percent to 30 percent commission on sales, which comes to earnings of Rs 15,000 to 20,000 in a month.

> *"Progress is a choice. Job creation is a choice. Whether we give our children a future of more or a future of less – this, too, is a choice."*
> – Martin O'Malley

Startups: Goldmine For Job Creation

Your job decides your livelihood, and in turn, pronounces a greater verdict on your life. Entrepreneurship is not only about filling your own pockets with profits; it is a responsible endeavor toward your people, your society, and your country. Startups are an amalgamation of passions and dreams to bring in a change in the existing system. Entrepreneurs are radically different in their perspectives; however, they all possess the commonality of determination to envision a better society and a prosperous country. It is never wrong to consider startups as the goldmines for job creation as they are the true interlopers of the monotony. One of the greatest examples of a startup becoming a goldmine of job creation is none other than Dhirubhai Ambani's Reliance—an ode to courage and perseverance.

Over the next decade, India's GDP must grow by 8 percent to 8.5 percent annually or about double the 4.2 percent rate of growth in the fiscal year 2020, to combat unemployment. Sectors like manufacturing and construction are likely to contribute one-fifth of incremental GDP to 2030. Similarly, construction could add one-fourth of the increments in jobs.

ENTREPRENEURSHIP EPIDEMIC

India has over 600 large firms with more than $500 million in revenue that generate 40 percent of all exports. While large firms contributed 48 percent of total GDP in 2018, we need to reach 70 percent contribution in line with outperforming economies. Thus, India has to triple the number of large firms. Then why should a country like India concentrate on startups? Startups are the architect of our growth. Consider a case scenario of a simple startup in the IT sector. At the initial stage itself, the startup creates around 10 to 15 jobs, which further leads to indirect jobs in the form of vendors, delivery partners for e-commerce, and SMM teams. A rise in entrepreneurship in India is like a launchpad for dynamic job creation.

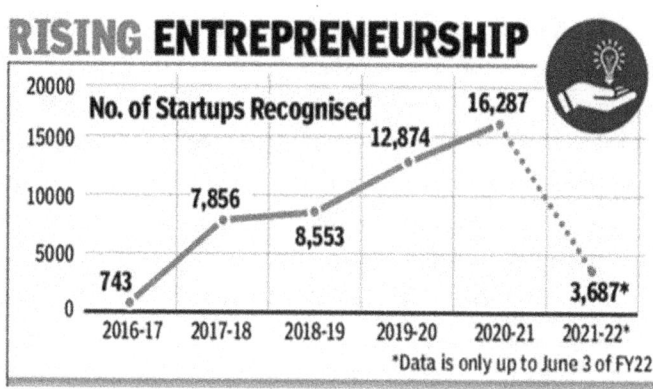

(Ref: DPIIT)

Through the Startup India initiative, there are around 50,000 startups registered, which have created over 5.5 lakh jobs. The different venture capitalists have played a key role in bolstering the startup ecosystem in India and helped in creating more than 3 million jobs directly or indirectly over the past eight years. There are a number of startups that have connected rural India with services and solutions to address grassroots-level issues and drive large-scale job creation through innovation and technology. According to the Department for Promotion of Industry and Internal Trade (DPIIT), startups in India have created over 560,000 jobs till now.

The direct jobs created by startups are estimated at 187,004, which has led to indirect employment opportunities for three lakhs more people. Considering 35 percent of the country's population consists of youth, growing unemployment is a daunting prospect, to say the least. With a growing population of young, educated, and qualified people, the job hunt has become increasingly desperate. Startup businesses, in this scenario, can play a pivotal role in shaping India's employment condition.

Even if you start a small business, it will encompass several tasks and responsibilities. Delegation of roles by an entrepreneur paves the first step of job creation. As an entrepreneur, you will have to hire someone to assist you while setting up the company. And as your business grows and expands, you will require both direct and indirect involvement from others. From a job seeker's perspective, it is easier to secure jobs in startups and small companies as giant firms have their own set of complex and often intimidating norms.

Startups speak for growth and innovation, and thus offer a lucrative career option for the younger breed. They prefer joining a new company and getting associated right from its inception stage. Startups are more involved in experimenting and diversifying, and the younger generations are finding it more comfortable. They all become a part in establishing their own work culture and as the company starts expanding, they become indispensable for they have been in the making right from its cradle. Job loss becomes rare in small companies. However, as Steve Jobs once said, *"When you are in a startup, the first ten people will determine whether your company succeeds or not."*

On this podium of the vulnerable job market, startups have become the only solution to rising unemployment. While they develop the required entrepreneurial skills in the youth and create numerous employment opportunities for deserving and needy candidates, startups are becoming the manure for the country's economic growth. Startups open the door to freelancers without creating the hassles of allowances and fringe benefits.

With the country's population increasing at an alarming rate, it is becoming more difficult to secure a stable job with every passing day. In such a situation, startups have come up to rescue and empower youth.

During the COVID-19 pandemic, BYJU'S, and their recently acquired coding learning platform WhiteHat Jr, could create over 20,000 job opportunities in the last six months. The edtech platforms have been on a hiring spree, onboarding more than 11,000 women, all of whom are working from home.

"The real way for India to become a superpower is with more entrepreneurs who create more employment."
– Nithin Kamath

The Startup Playground of India

India has been a booming economy during the revolutionary advances in the IT sector. Shiv Nadar and Narayan Murthy, among many others, had crafted this entire niche for Indians to look for opportunities. As time passed by, Jeff Bezos threw us into another dimension to explore and e-commerce brought in the new dawn. The idea of entrepreneurship gained momentum gradually and today India has some of the startups minting money through their unique business ideas and marketing strategies. The following have been the fastest-growing startups in India.

The startup playground is huge and is growing from every nook and corner. And while opening new doors of employment, many sectors have been overpowered by others.

> **Information Technology**: Irrespective of the Covid-19 economic downturn, the IT sector has consistently generated employment. According to NASSCOM, in FY21, the Indian tech sector was expected to add 1.38 lakh jobs. Interestingly, startup creation in the tech sector is consistently high.

Nearly 1,600 startups were added in FY21, leading to increased opportunities for job creation.

- **E-commerce**: The internet user statistics shall support the growth in this sector. People are more adopted to online shopping now and thus more startups shall be launched to deal with the growing demand. Online stores such as Amazon and Flipkart have generated $4.1 billion in sales during the festive season in 2020, compared to $2.7 billion in 2019. The sector has added 300,000 jobs in 2021.
- **Healthcare**: With the increased need for healthcare services during the pandemic, there was a huge demand–supply gap in this sector. Also, the situation highlighted that a lot needs to be done to build a more robust healthcare ecosystem. NSDC estimates that the healthcare sector will create 7.5 million jobs by 2022.
- **Infrastructure**: India's construction sector is a major source of employment and directly affects government policy. It may be fragmented and unorganized; however, a more favorable fiscal policy that encourages infrastructure development will eventually lead to increased employment.

According to a study conducted by Praxis Global Alliance, startups are growing at an average rate of 12 percent to 15 percent annually. India is in the middle of a startup revolution and from 2016 to 2020, has raised around $63 billion in funding. Investments in startups have grown incrementally with each passing year at $16.7. Start-Up India somehow kick-started an entrepreneurship revolution through a number of policy interventions.

The overhaul of the digital payments' ecosystem is being led by State innovation, with Aadhaar, Jan Dhan, UPI, and India Stack. The Atal Innovation Mission, Niti Aayog, has built an ecosystem of 8,800 tinkering labs, 4,000 mentors, and over two-and-a-half million students, and also acted as a channel for over 3,500 innovations.

In fact, the National Education Policy 2020 focuses on student entrepreneurs by offering vocational education in partnership with industries and introducing coding for schoolchildren. Similarly, the National Digital Health Mission presents opportunities for health-tech startups. The new farm acts have chalked out a greater choice to farmers and incentivized startups to transform the agriculture value chain in storage, finance, transport, aggregation, and marketing.

"Indian entities can undertake design, development and realization of satellites and associated communication systems. They can establish satellite system through their own built satellite or procured satellite."
— Draft Space Policy (2020)

A number of reforms are going on while widening the scope of startups in India. FIA Global has a network of 26,000 banking agents and is using Artificial Intelligence (AI) to deliver financial products and services such as remittance services and access to credit in rural areas. So far, it has reached over 34 million customers. A digital bookkeeping startup such as OKCredit is helping micro-merchants in maintaining paperless and secure transaction profiles, with a multilingual app.

Can you believe that around 5.5 million merchants are reaping the benefits? Similarly, MFine provides an AI-powered healthcare platform for people to consult over 3,500 doctors. BYJU'S has become a household name by benefitting over 70 million students. Camp K12 is taking coding lessons to the children in rural areas.

India has been witnessing a significant change after embracing technology in every stratum of business. DeHaat's end-to-end services, from advisory services, distribution of agricultural inputs, access to financial services, and market linkages have been utilized by 2, 65,000 farmers in Bihar, Uttar Pradesh, and Odisha. It has helped in savings of up to 15 percent on agriculture inputs, raised productivity by 20 percent, and increased farmers' incomes up to 50 percent.

The startup named Pixxel is building a constellation of satellites to detect and evaluate high-quality data. It will use AI/ML for predictive and productivity-enhancing mechanisms in agriculture, climate change, and mining. Bellatrix Aerospace envisions making access to space more economical and secure by developing its own launch vehicles named Chetak and electric propulsion systems. Innovative entrepreneurs of India are riding on a resilient policy system and are utilizing unprecedented advances in technology. India's startup ecosystem is operating on the demands of our demography, and inadvertently steering out new strategies to widen the scopes.

Is Zero Investment Really Possible?

As the well-known proverb goes, 'All that glitters is not gold.' Every business requires some sort of investment if it wants to grow. Aggressive moves in business indeed need a lot of funding. However, if you fail to acquire any capital to invest in the beginning, there is still a ray of hope. There lie a couple of doors open to start a business at a slower pace with zero investment.

> - **Blogging:** There are a plethora of options available here as everyone is surfing through the net for information. You can always start a blog of your own, free of investment. All you need is to be focused, diligent, and simply famous to make money through blogging. Remember, blogging is about creating content to get money. Thus, it becomes imperative for you to understand the concept of SEO. By blogging about a specific topic of your interest, you can pull in readers or traffic, which in turn can translate into money. There are various ways in which you can earn through a blog or vlog on YouTube, such as ad placements via Google AdSense. You can opt for affiliate marketing by promoting others' products on your blog, doing product reviews, guest posts in others' blogs, or product sales on your blog.

- **Travel Agency:** There is a considerable desire for travel these days and many are struck by wanderlust; however, there are never enough resources for meticulous planning. So, if you have a fervor for travel, this profession can make you rich. Like a good travel agent, you must be able to plan a great itinerary for clients that offers superb arrangements in the most pocket-friendly way. There is no initial startup cost for opening a travel agency, other than getting a high-speed internet connection. If you have authentic knowledge of historical facts, you may become a tour guide for your clients and travel with them to breathtaking locales around the world.
- **Tiffin Service:** There is no better recession-proof business than a tiffin service. It has turned out to be a profitable startup with low investment, especially for women, as the 'eating out' trend has been replaced with 'eating in'. And whilst most of the young Indian couples are working, the demand for tiffin service has increased manifold. People are willing to pay well for a healthy tiffin service.
- **Online Fitness Instructor:** Becoming an online fitness instructor is a new rage today and the business is growing wider after the pandemic. If you are a fitness freak, you simply need to upload your fitness tutorials on social media and get people to follow you there. If you are good at your work, you can easily establish a strong online presence and become a great fitness instructor without renting any studio space.
- **Event Management:** Another recession-proof business in India is event management. There is no dearth of big fat Indian weddings, ceremonies, and grand parties in India. Planning an event, either on a professional or personal scale, requires looking after minute details to make it super successful. If you have a panache for creativity and the right networking, the event management business is the right choice for you.

- **DIY Home Decors:** Such quirky pieces made of unconventional ideas amuse people from all walks of life. If you have a tint of creativity and a like-minded workforce, you can come up with such projects on an experimental basis initially.
- **Online Selling:** If you are a professional artist, or good at any form of art, online selling is a good option. Facebook marketplace, Amazon, Flipkart, etc., provide ample opportunities for small-scale businesses.
- **Become a YouTuber or Insta-influencer:** It is one of the most popular business plans in India with zero investments.
- **Consulting Services:** An experienced person is an ocean of knowledge. Budding professionals and startup business owners often hire freelancers for their expertise. Consulting is a service that costs only time to produce but can be highly valuable as a career opportunity.
- **Resale:** There are two options to this: drop-shipping or wholesaling to acquire these goods. With drop-shipping, you will ship directly from the manufacturer and will not need much startup cash. With wholesaling, you will need more money and space up-front, but would also earn more money.
- **Micropreneurship:** It is more of a shared economy opportunity: much like renting out your home to OYO Rooms or your car to Uber.
- **Content Writing:** Content has become the king. Whether for making a blockbuster movie or for marketing a startup business, content writing jobs are ruling the market.
- **Online Surveys:** Possibly one of the easiest ways to earn money is through paid online surveys. Swagbucks is among the most well-known sites and pays for participating in several activities like filling out surveys, watching videos, and shopping, among others.
- **Online Tutoring:** If you are academically gifted, you can earn by teaching or selling courses on online platforms.

> **Storytelling via Podcasts:** If you are good at oratory and love telling stories, monetize your skill.

These low investment business ideas in India prove that capital can never be a roadblock on your journey to start a business. Moreover, there is never a downside to a side hustle. Your present job can be your primary source of income, and you can still slowly get into the shoes of an entrepreneur.

A Thought To Network Marketing/Direct Selling

Any small-scale business grows and prospers through word of mouth. Building a network of people who talk about your business is one of the essential ingredients for weaving your success. While you ponder upon the correlation between your capital and business career, I suggest you lend a thought to network marketing. The crux of network marketing is to build people who in turn build your business. It is a business model that depends on person-to-person sales by independent representatives who more often work from home. It is like building a network of business partners or salespeople to assist with lead generation and closing sales.

Network marketing is often known as affiliate marketing, multilevel marketing, consumer-direct marketing, referral marketing, or home-based business franchising. Companies that follow the network marketing model create tiers of salespeople by encouraging them to recruit their own networks of salespeople. The one who creates the new tier earns a commission on not only their own sales but also on the sales made by the others in the tier they created. As and when a new tier sprouts yet another tier, it contributes more commission to the person in the top tier as well as the middle tier.

Thus, the earnings of salespeople depend on recruitment as well as product sales. Similarly, those who have got in early stay at a top tier and make the most. Network marketing is alluring as an individual with a lot of energy and good sales skills can create a profitable business with a modest investment.

But, Beware of Pyramid Schemes! The salespeople in the top tier can make impressive amounts of money on commissions from the tiers below them. The people on the lower tiers will earn much less. In pyramid schemes, the company makes money by selling expensive starter kits to new recruits. But all said and done, making money out of network marketing is certainly possible. Some people enjoy great success at network marketing because of their ability to recruit more members to the network. They earn from two main revenue sources: by selling products and from commissions on sales made by team members downline. The more people there are downline from you, the more money you will accumulate. Similarly, the larger the team you can recruit, the more money you can make.

It has been found that most people who join legitimate network marketing programs make little or no money. Some may lose money or may become involved in an illegal pyramid scheme and not realize that they have joined a fraudulent venture, and can lose everything they invest. Before indulging in network marketing, do your research.

Amway has been the top-grossing network marketing program. Top-selling brands for Amway are Nutrilite vitamin, mineral, and dietary supplements, Artistry skincare and color cosmetics, eSpring water treatment systems, and XS energy drinks; all these are sold exclusively by independent Amway Business Owners. In 2020 alone it brought in $8.5 billion in revenue.

Modicare founded by Sameer Modi is one of the fastest developing Indian network marketing companies in the nation. It offers a wide range of items from categories like Wellness, Skin Care, Personal care, Homecare, and so forth. As a Modicare consultant, you can purchase items at a 20 percent to 25 percent cheaper rate and sell them with a 25 percent margin. Consultants with higher sales volumes are awarded Power Seller Bonus, which can be between 5 percent and 20 percent based on the business volume. Direct selling and network marketing open the doors to business opportunities for almost everyone.

Irrespective of your educational background, skills, and capital worth, you are absolutely eligible to dive into the world of business. With relatively less investment and low overheads, the direct selling or network marketing business model is flexible and creates a good amount of passive income. And while thinking of women empowerment, network marketing or direct selling has been a boon to them. As Art Jonak quoted, *"Direct selling is one of the few places where women earn dollar for dollar what men earn."*

Electric Vehicle Market Is Sprouting

Well! If startups are bound to focus on an existing problem, there is no bigger threat than climate change and greenhouse gas emissions. Electric vehicle (EV) has come up as the only option for easy transportation without affecting the environment much. The Indian EV revolution has somehow come to a halt due to the Covid-19 lockdown. The mobility sector, which is a massive customer base for EV manufacturers, has been harmed heavily. To promote the adoption of EVs in the country, the Indian government has announced a new policy and initiative that may help India to adopt an EV Environment quickly.

"The intensity of impact will be much sharper in the electric vehicle segment"
– Sohinder Gill, CEO, Hero electric

Globally, the EV sector has become the fastest-growing job creator and India has to encroach into this sector strategically. Since the 20th century, the automobile sector has been the wealth generator for most of the global economies. With technological intervention, growth and extension became a constant in the evolution of the automobile industry. Globalization resulted in an increase in domestic production and job and value creation. None can deny the prominent role played by the auto sector in the economic output of India—comprising about half of the manufacturing GDP and seven percent of the overall GDP.

Moreover, this sector employs over 35 million of India's workforce, both directly and indirectly. The automobile sector leaves a huge footprint on livelihood creation. However, according to a report published by News18.com, there has been a paradigm shift in the employment status by 2020. About 3,50,000 people were laid off due to the scheduled leapfrogging to BS-VI norms for emission control and the thrust on EVs to achieve high electrification by 2030. However, the future is not totally dark. In our pursuit of a sustainable future, there are plenty of EV jobs around.

This is to note that several entrepreneurial initiatives on the EV pathway have surfaced at the nick of the competing ecosystem. For example, Ather Energy is planning to set up a manufacturing unit in south India with an investment to the tune of $50 to $100 million, while Mahindra Electric has invested Rs 100 crore last year for a manufacturing plant in Bengaluru. India claims over a healthy mix of new-age startups and legacy Original Equipment Manufacturers (OEMs). The latter showing interest in the technology of the future also provides the necessary impetus to drive skilling initiatives. The burgeoning scope in EV shall be able to puff a new lease of life into skilled workers of the auto industry. This initiative of upskilling is going to serve as a comforting cushion for the skilled laborers in the automobile sector.

India has been the hub for automobile manufacturing in South Asia and is the fourth largest auto market in the world. With several investors and venture capitalists in the startup ecosystem, we can be a strong launchpad to transition to EVs and be a leader. As the world is focusing on EVs, this particular sector seems to be the gap we have to bridge. There prevails a wide scope of opportunities in the segment of design and testing, wiring harnesses, manufacturing and management, sales, services, technology for battery, automation, smart mobility, infrastructure for charging/swapping, and making the existing building infrastructure EV-ready. The government's initiative to be vocal for local manufacturing shall help in creating an indigenous EV supply chain in the country.

Moreover, as the tax rate has been lowered to 15 percent on new manufacturing companies, private investments are pouring in. Manufacturing of tropical EVs and batteries are on the rise as EV's must be made suitable for the Indian environment. The evolution of ICE technology is helping out in retrofitting the existing vehicles. Further research and innovation in chemical and materials engineering and mineral mining are spinning out new opportunities to look into by the startups. Do you know that Indian states like Uttar Pradesh, Telangana, Tamil Nadu, and Kerala have redesigned the academic curriculum of engineering and polytechnic colleges and ITIs to suit the EV industry requirements? Electric vehicle or E-mobility space has several domains to work upon and thus there exist a plethora of opportunities for the new breed of entrepreneurs.

Let us have a brief look at how different domains of the EV sector have been prospering.

Manufacturing Segment: It was initially a big hurdle to cross and enter the space of manufacturing EVs. Ather Energy, Ultraviolette, Emflux motors, and a few more have triumphed over and introduced a new wave of startup ideas. In the scope of battery assembly, India imports the cells from Taiwan or China, and Indian companies like PuREnergy and Renon India assemble the cells into battery packs and supply them to the OEMs. In fact, as a part of the circular economy, there are a few startups like Ziptrax and Raasi Solar that streamline the lifecycle management of the batteries.

Presently, India imports powertrain components. However, there are several startups that are focused on R&D to improve the efficiency and performance of the powertrain while customizing it to the Indian conditions. Altigreen Propulsion Labs, Virya mobility, and Elecnovo are some of the startups that are ruling the market. In fact, established companies like TVS Lucas have diversified into the EV sector. Similarly, Delta electronics and Exicom are occupied with manufacturing the charging equipment.

- **Software Development:** The concept of EV has introduced an opportunity in the scope of telematics solutions, software for vehicle performance simulation, and operating systems. Companies like eMotive Systems, REVOS, and Esmito provide a B2B Saas platform for EV infrastructure management.
- **Charging Infrastructure Segment:** EVs need charging networks in public places. Established players like NTPC, REIL, and EESL are accompanied by startups like Charge+Zone (Vadodara), Volttic, and Magenta Chargegrid.
- **Swapping Solutions:** Battery swapping is an essential factor in the maintenance of EVs. Startups like Sun Mobility and E-Chargeup Solutions are building a brighter future in this scope.
- **Training Sector:** EV has brought in a revolution, and to move into the space smoothly, training and skill development remain crucial factors. Many startups like Autobot India and DIY Guru are knitting success tales by providing training to skilled workers.
- **Retrofitting:** While combating the climate change issue, you cannot undo the already manufactured vehicles. Thus, companies like Trio and BharatMobi are focused on converting ICE vehicles to Electric or Hybrid vehicles. Do you know Gati delivers IKEA products in Hyderabad using electric 3Ws and retrofitted TATA Ace?
- **Electric Bike Rentals:** Micro-mobility and daily commutes are gaining momentum as companies like Yulu Bikes and Bounce are looking for franchise partners in different cities.

Lithium-ion Battery Recycling Segment: In 2019, the global lithium-ion battery recycling market size was USD 1.31 billion and it has seen a spectacular growth of 20.1 percent in 2020 and by 2027, it shall grow to USD 11.07 billion. The fast-growing global EV market is indirectly boosting the lithium-ion battery recycling business and this could be a great business opportunity for the startups. In short, the small-scale industries can look into the following business opportunities in the EV Sector:

- Public Charging stations
- A Battery Energy Storage System (BESS)
- Recycling lithium-ion batteries Plant
- A solar photo voltaic-powered EV
- Battery Management System (BMS)
- Battery Swapping Plant
- EV charging Software

Case Study: The zero-emission EV charging station powered by solar cell

A solar photo voltaic-powered electric vehicle (EV) charging station has been developed at the Indian Institute of Science (IISc) in Bangalore tech city.

This solar charging station consists of EV supply equipment (EVSE), an array of solar panels, an inverter to convert solar power from DC to AC, an energy storage system (for off-grid charging),

> *With my personal inclination towards sustainable living and environmental-friendly technology, my group, Somika SARL has invested in TecSo ChargeZone, a company based out of Vadodara. Somika group is also setting up EV Battery Cell Precursor, Cathode Active Material and Cathode plant in Bharuch District of Gujarat within PCPIR zone in collaboration with Special Purpose Vehicle -Infinite Elements Pvt. Ltd.*

charge controllers, and a secure network for the wireless transmission of data to help users make real-time decisions. If you have a minimum of ₹ 5 million, you can get on board and stay invested as this industry is going to progress.

The drive toward green energy, sustainable living, and EVs is creating a myriad of opportunities for the new breed of entrepreneurs. You can take the first step by engaging in dealer/distributorship for the existing brands. Many startups like Sun Mobility and Yulu Bikes are looking for franchises in different cities. The concept of EVs has introduced a radical shift in the business world and this e-mobility space is yet to be explored further.

"You don't need to chase wealth, just become a real entrepreneur and the world is your oyster."
– Amah Lambert

Key Takeaways:

- Money is not a roadblock to starting a business.
- Learn the different scopes in India to plunge into business.
- Understand how electric vehicle space is an emerging option.

10

FIND A GENUINE INVESTOR

The year 2021 has sewn a new thread of optimism as the startup ecosystem crossed 100 billion USD of investment.

The present times have proven that investors are no longer afraid to take risks and test new waters. Startup funding is becoming an increasingly frequent headline these days and you, as an entrepreneur, must not gripe over the missed boat. As an early-stage entrepreneur, it is crucial for you to be aware of big investment deals in your niche so that you can incorporate them into your pitch. With technology evolving at a faster rate and brighter ideas cropping up at every corner, investors are now open to newer and challenging domains. They are willing to give an opportunity to entrepreneurs who carry the potential to become the catalysts of change in the entrepreneurial milieu.

Investors have a key role as one of the main players in the process of funding. Their expertise and involvement are determinants of a funded venture's success. This makes it imperative for entrepreneurs to know everything about the different investors present in the market and pitch their proposals to the right investor.

Most Active Angel Investors In India

With social media gaining prominence, getting in touch with an angel investor has become easier than ever. Some of the most active angel investors are listed below along with their preferred sectors.

Angel Investor	Preferred Sector	Invested In
Amit Lakhotia	Fintech, Social commerce platform	BharatPe, Trell, GoKwick, Junio
Amrish Rau	Fintech	Locus, Multiplier, OneCode. (Rau has invested in more than 35 startups)
Anand Chandrasekharan	Cloud management, B2B ecommerce platform	OpsLyft, SuperK, Venwiz
Anupam Mittal	Technology, Consumer Internet, Mobile Health Care	HackerEarth, Drivezy, Kae Capital, Ola Cabs
Anjali Bansal	Mulifaceted – Tech brands to cosmetics	Darwinbox, Nykaa, Lenskart, Mudrex, Qapita
Anuj Srivastava	Home décor, healthtech, lifestyle brand	Nestasia, Nirogstreet
Apoorva Sharma	Multifaceted (Fintech, AI, Edtech, Hospitality)	OYO, Beardo (More than 100+ startups were curated, incubated and mentored
Binny Bansal	Fintech, Edtech	PlanetSpark, Skill

		Lync, and fintech startup Rupifi.
Deep Kalra	Healthtech, Edtech	eka.care, PlanetSpark
Deepinder Goyal	Healthtech, HRtech, B2B ecommerce	Pristyn Care, Multiplier, Geniemode, Unacademy, Bira 91, Animall.
Dheeraj Jain (Redcliff Capital)	AI, Virtual Reality, Big Data Analytics, Healthcare, Biotechnology	Mapper, Burger Singh, ShaadiSaga, Qdesq, Deyor
Gaurav Munjal	Edtech, Healthtech	AdmitKard, eka.care
Girish Mathrubhootham	Edtech, Saas, tech enabled sales	Newton School, Oslash, GTM Buddy
Harshil Mathur	B2B trading, Edtech, ecommerce	GlobalFair, Newton School, OneCode
Jitendra Gupta	Health-tech, D2C brands, tech infrastructure	Lets Hash, Meddo Health, Hypto
Kunal Shah	Fintech, ecommerce, SaaS	Niro, OneCode, Onsurity.
Kunal Bahl and Rohit Bansal (Titan Capital)	Construction, Edtech, Transport market place	Powerplay, Questt, Vahak
Miten Sampat	Multifaceted	OneCode, Onsurity, RAAHO,
Naveen Tewari	Coworking Spaces, Online	Wooplr, Springboard,

	Games, Technology	Razorpay, LetsVenture, Mettl
Rajesh Sawhney (GSF Accelerator)	Fintech, Edtech, Construction	Paisagrowth, NxtWave, Kolo (More than 100 startups funded)
Ramakant Sharma	Crypto exchange, Fintech	CoinSwitch Kuber, Slice (More than 50 startups funded till date)
Rajan Anandan	Big data Analytics, Healthcare, Mobile commerce, Digital media	Instamojo, TravelKhana, SocialCops
Ratan Tata	Technology Sector, E-commerce, Affiliate Sectors	Xiaomi, Urban Ladder, NestAway, One97 Communications, Invictus Oncology, Idea Chakki
Sachin Bansal	Saas, Internet services, Analytics and AI, Online commerce	Unacademy, Inshorts, Ather Energy, SigTuple
Sandeep Tandon	Internet Services, Fintech, Healthcare, Education	Razorpay, Inc42, Tablehero, Unacademy, Fabelio
Sanjay Mehta	Clean Technology, Enterprise Software, healthcare	LogiNext, LawRato, OYO, Box8

TV Mohan Das Pai	Technology startups, Consumer internet, Media	Zoomcar, Zimmber, YourStory, FairCent
Vijay Shekhar Sharma	Fintech, Edtech, Consumer Internet	Unacademy, GOQii, Flyrobe, Milaap
Zishaan Hayath	Ed Tech, Saas Products	Shadowfax, SquadRun, Wealthy

FAQ

1. **How can I connect with angel investors in India?**
   Browse through social media channels like LinkedIn or special apps like Angelists, Lestventure, etc.

2. **Who are the most active startup angel investor networks?**
   Apart from the above-mentioned list, one can check for websites of Venture Catalysts or Indian Angel Network..

Venture Capitalists In India

The year 2021 has seen Indian startups successfully managing to gather $36 billion worth of funds. While angel investors did their role, most of the funding came through VC firms. The past few years have seen a steep rise in VC firms' investment in Indian startups, thereby helping gear up the Indian startup ecosystem. Venture Catalysts is India's first integrated incubator which is founded by Dr. Apoorva Ranjan Sharma. Venture Catalysts has been ranked world's 7th Largest Incubator and Early-Stage Investor by TechCrunch in 2019. Dr. Apoorva Sharma is one of the founding fathers of the startup ecosystem in India and has been a pioneer in establishing incubators in India.

He has established over a dozen incubators and accelerators, incubation funds and family office funds like Amity Innovation Incubator, Somaiya Incubator, Mata Vaishno Devi University Incubator, and Indian Angel Network Incubator. In the past two decades, Dr. Sharma has curated, incubated and led seed investment of 100+ startups in which OYO Rooms has been the biggest success story followed by Beardo. Both the startups were curated, mentored and seed sourced by Dr. Apoorva Sharma.

Apart from homegrown, Venture Catalysts and 9Unicorns, there are many top venture capitalists working throughout India and are helping Indian Startups leave their footprints on the global landscape.

Sequoia Capital

Notable Investments	Apple, Google, Oracle, Nvidia, GitHub, PayPal, LinkedIn, Stripe, Bird, YouTube, Instagram, Yahoo!, PicsArt, Klarna, and WhatsApp
Key Sectors	Agnostic
Stage	Early Stage, Late Stage, Seed Stage
Website	www.sequoiacap.com

Accel

Notable Investments	Freshworks, Swiggy, BlackBuck, Bounce, BookMyShow, Flipkart
Key Sectors	Agnostic
Stage	Early Stage, Late Stage, Seed Stage
Subsidiaries	ACCEL PARTNERS LIMITED, Accel Partners Management LLP
Website	www.accel.com

Blume Ventures

Notable Investments	Dunzo, Unacademy, Instamojo, Procol, HealthAssure, Milkbasket
Key Sectors	Agnostic
Stage	Early Stage, Seed Stage
Website	www.blume.vc

Elevation Capital

Notable Investments	Capital Float, Firstcry, Swiggy, IndustryBuying, Aye Finance, Rivigo, Cleartax
Key Sectors	Agnostic
Stage	Stage Agnostic, Private Equity
Website	www.elevationcapital.com

Tiger Global Management

Notable Investments	Urban Company, Flipkart, Moglix, OPEN, Ninjacart, Razorpay
Key Sectors	Internet, Software, Consumer, Financial Technology
Stage	Growth, Late Stage, Private Equity, Post-IPO
Website	www.tigerglobal.com

Kalaari Capital

Notable Investments	CashKaro, CureFit, WinZO, Jumbotail, Milkbasket, Myntra, Snapdeal
Key Sectors	Agnostic
Stage	Early Stage
Website	www.kalaari.com

Matrix Partners

Notable Investments	Avail Finance, Vogo, DailyNinja, Stanza Living, MoEngage
Key Sectors	Agnostic
Stage	Early Stage Venture, Seed
Website	www.matrixpartners.com

Nexus Venture Partners

Notable Investments	WhiteHat Jr, Delhivery, Rapido, Unacademy, Druva, Jumbotail, Bolo App, Pratilipi, Zomato
Key Sectors	Agnostic
Stage	Early Stage, Seed Stage
Website	www.nexusvp.com

Indian Angel Network

Notable Investments	WebEngage, Wow! Momo, Dhruva, Box8, FabAlley, Little Black Book
Key Sectors	Agnostic
Stage	Early Stage, Seed Stage
Website	www.indianangelnetwork.com

Omidyar Network India

Notable Investments	Dailyhunt, Indifi Technologies, 1mg, Needslist, Bounce, Platzi, Pratilipi, HealthKart, Doubtnut, ZestMoney, WhiteHat Education Technology
Key Sectors	Agnostic
Stage	Early Stage, Seed Stage
Website	www.omidyarnetwork.in

Venture Catalysts

Notable Investments	7 Classes, AgriGator, Algobulls, BharatPe, Beardo, Callify.ai, Charge Zone, Cusmat, DSYH
Key Sectors	Agnostic
Stage	Early Stage, Seed Stage
Website	www.venturecatalysts.in

9UNICORNS

Notable Investments	Toch, DeepSync, Klub, Mitron, Oga, Tamasha, Janani AI, NeoDocs, Instoried, Humus
Key Sectors	Agnostic (16,500 startups curated)
Stage	Early Stage
Website	www.9unicorns.in

Securing funds has never been easier before. Here is a comprehensive list of all the active venture capitalist firms in India.

Company Name	Get In Touch
Accel	accel.com
ah! Ventures	ahventures.in
Amicus Capital, L.P.	amicuscapital.in
Ankur Capital Fund	ankurcapital.com
Aspada	aspada.com
Augment Ventures	augmentventures.com
Axilor Ventures	axilor.com
Blume Ventures	blume.vc
Brand Capital, India	brandcapital.co.in
Canaan	Canaan.com
Chiratae Ventures	chiratae.com
Crowdcube	www.crowdcube.com

Eight Roads	eightroads.com
Elevar Equity	elevarequity.com
Equanimity Investments	equanimityinvestments.com
Firstround capital	firstround.com
FOSUN RZ Capital	frzcapital.cn
Gaja Capital	gajacapital.com
General Atlantic LLC	generalatlantic.com
General Catalyst Partners	generalcatalyst.com
Green Shoots Capital	greenshootscapital.co.in
growX ventures	growxventures.com
Helion Advisors Pvt. Ltd.	helionvc.com
Indian Angel Network	indianangelnetwork.com
Inventus Capital Partners	inventuscap.com
ITI Growth Opportunities Fund	itigo.in
IvyCap Ventures Pvt Ltd	ivycapventures.com
Jungle Ventures	jungle-ventures.com
Kae Capital	kae-capital.com
Kalaari	kalaari.com
Khosla Ventures	khoslaventures.com
LetsVenture	letsventure.com
Mayfield Fund	mayfield.com
Menlo Ventures	menlovc.com
Menterra Ventures	menterra.com
Nair Ventures	nairventures.com
Naspers	naspers.com
Nexus Venture Partners	nexusvp.com
Norwest Venture Partners	nvp.com
Omnivore	omnivore.vc
Orios Venture Partners	oriosvp.com
Pravega Ventures	pravegavc.com
Qualcomm Ventures	qualcommventures.com
Quona Capital	quona.com
Rockstud Capital	rockstudcap.com

SAIF Partners	saifpartners.com
Sequoia Capital India	sequoiacap.com
Sistema Asia Capital India	sistemaasiacapital.com
Sixth Sense Ventures	sixth-sense.in
Sprout Venture Partners	sproutvp.com
Steadview Capital	steadview.com
Stellaris Venture Partners	stellarisvp.com
Tracxn	tracxn.com
Trifecta Capital Advisors	trifectacapital.in
Venture Catalysts	Venturecatalysts.in
Zodius Capital	zodius.com
500 Startups	500.co
8i Ventures	8i.vc
9UNICORNS	9unicorns.in

FAQs

1. **Is there any database where I can find all the funding agencies?**

   Yes. Venture Intelligence is India's first private equity and venture capital transaction database. One can visit their website www.ventureintelligence.com for all the details.

2. **Which VC firm will suit my business the most?**

   It depends on the stage and sector of the startup. Venture Capitalist firms are generally agnostic toward sectors and more focused on the stage. Do the research while checking credibility.

Lastly, I would say money is no longer a hurdle. If your idea is great, there is always a helping hand round the corner.

CONCLUSION

Despite the dreariness, despair, and despondency that an entrepreneur feels while navigating through the challenges, choosing business as a career is worth it. Every business, traditional or startup, is bound to go through a lot of ups and downs. However, hard work and willingness to endure success and failure construct the backbone of a successful business. As the breadwinner of the family, you will likely face a lot of familial and societal pressures to opt for a more secure and stable job. Encounters with naysayers may become more frequent in life, but as soon as you realize your true purpose in running a business, you understand your worth. Considering the current job market, choosing business as a career seems more lucrative. Apart from becoming self-reliant, you will be contributing to the job market as well.

However, if your educational background is making you hesitant to take the plunge, then fear not. It is your salesman skills, storytelling abilities, and field experience that hone your prospects as a businessman. Entrepreneurship is about identifying an existing problem and disrupting the problem with an innovative strategy—be it a new product or service. Understand what kind of business model is suitable for you, go for the partners who share your passion and values, and dive into the world of business.

But before you try your hand in entrepreneurship, learn about the startup ecosystem and how to choose the most suitable sector in the burgeoning Indian market. The startup journey is not a cakewalk. It needs 24/7 dedication with firm knowledge about the requirements. One of the biggest hurdles comes in the form of choosing the right cofounders. One must acknowledge the significance of diversity in the organizational structure. The presence of diverse skills amongst the cofounders is an asset for the growth of any business. And as the business propagates well, the dilemma appears in the scope of succession planning. If one wishes to prepare the business for the future, one can never overlook the idea of succession planning. Remember, your business is a source of income for your employees and that is why startups are called the goldmines of job creation. As India's startup ecosystem flourishes, several sectors like fintech, edtech, and internet services have become regular areas to explore. However, the electric vehicle space has gathered much attention recently for its role in combating the problem of climate change.

The present time is apt for taking the plunge into entrepreneurship. With regular evolution in technology, each day sees a new area to explore. And as investors are no longer afraid to try out something new, anyone can step into the shoes of an entrepreneur by learning the tactics of the game. Startups are not only about a different idea; it is about transforming the idea into something for everyone's good. Running a business is not about dreaming of brimful coffers; it is about pure perseverance and persistence. And before I leave you to knit your passion for business, read through Jeff Bezos's words,

"I knew that if I failed, I wouldn't regret that, but I knew the one thing I might regret is not trying."

References

1.

- https://www.investopedia.com/terms/s/startup.asp
- https://www.mbacrystalball.com/blog/2016/03/23/best-age-to-start-business/
- https://sugermint.com/sanjeev-bikhchandani-naukri-com-founder-of/
- https://startuptalky.com/zomato-success-story/

2

- https://theceostory.in/blog/dhirubhai-ambani/
- https://online.maryville.edu/business-degrees/traditional-types-business-models/
- https://www.indiatechdesk.com/top-5-popular-startup-sectors-in-india/
- https://www.teamleader.eu/blog/sales-techniques
- https://lapaas.com/nykaa-business-model-detailed-case-study/

3

- https://youthmotivator4life.com/godrej/
- https://www.businesstoday.in/opinion/perspective/story/five-lessons-for-indian-business-from-hero-group-founder-brijmohan-lall-munjals-legacy-56378-2015-11-04
- https://www.bizencyclopedia.com/article/story-of-op-jindal-the-pioneer-in-the-indian-steel-industry
- https://www.arvind.com/arvind-story
- https://wirally.com/success-story-of-asian-paints/
- https://startuptalky.com/infosys-success-story/
- https://hcl.com/hcl-story/

4.

- https://www.startupindia.gov.in/content/sih/en/international/go-to-market-guide/indian-startup-ecosystem.html
- https://www.orfonline.org/research/the-indian-startup-ecosystem-drivers-challenges-and-pillars-of-support-55387/
- https://inc42.com/startups/

5

- https://startuptalky.com/big-basket/

6

- https://www.startupindia.gov.in/content/sih/en/funding.html
- https://www.bizencyclopedia.com/article/the-success-story-of-zoho-corporation
- https://www.analyticssteps.com/blogs/success-story-zerodha

7

- https://openstax.org/books/entrepreneurship/pages/10-2-why-early-failure-can-lead-to-success-later
- https://hellomeets.com/blog/failed-startups-of-india/

8

- CEO Succession Planning In India (https://www.ifc.org/wps

9.

- https://dpiit.gov.in/
- www.inc42.com
- https://e-vehicleinfo.com/business-opportunities-in-electric-vehicles-sector-in-india/

- https://evreporter.com/business-opportunities-in-ev-space/

10.

- https://inc42.com/features/the-32-most-active-angel-investors-for-indian-startups/
- https://digest.myhq.in/active-angel-investors-india/
- https://startuptalky.com/top-venture-capital-firms-india/
- https://ivca.in/